Wealth

A TORAH APPROACH

AVRAHAM TZVI SCHWARTZ

From the author of:
Hearts on Fire
Be Happy and Succeed

Copyright © 1997 - 2005, A. T. Schwartz

~~~~~~~~~~~~~~~~~~~~

MELECH PUBLICATIONS
MESHECH CHOCHMA 27/3,
MODIIN ELITE 71919, ISRAEL

WWW.BNPUBLISHING.COM

בס"ד מוצאי שבת קדש פ' בהר סיני

Ohr Lagolah
LEADERSHIP INSTITUTE

A Torah Corps
Training Program
for Educators and
Communal Leaders

Rabbi Nachman Bulman
Director

Rabbi Pesach Rosenzweig
Associate Director

an affiliate of
OHR SOMAYACH
Tanenbaum College

3 Tidhar Street
POB 18103
Jerusalem, 91180, Israel
Tel: 02-581-0315
Fax: 02-581-1890

American Friends of
OHR LAGOLAH
244 Madison Avenue
Suite 372
New York, NY 10016

To Whom It May Concern –

It is an honor and pleasure to introduce R. Tzvi Schwartz. R. Schwartz is a creative and inspiring Torah teacher and has in the recent past authored a precious work – "A Handful of Light" – on the "Letter of Ramban" – for which many are grateful to him. He is now ready to publish a work on Torah outlook on "Wealth" (having said one word as its title).

A quick glance at its contents discloses that "Wealth" is based on some five hundred citations from the teachers of our Sages. The work is sure to enrich unknown numbers of Jews at every level of Torah knowledge and interests. Since the subject is both vital and misunderstood, all who love Torah and the People-of-Torah will בע״ה be indebted to the author.

בברכת התורה וכל טוב, ובתודה; ובכבוד רב –
נחמן בולמן – הרב אברהם שרמן – אם אחיכם

RABBI ZEV LEFF
Rav of Moshav Matityahu
Rosh Hayeshiva
Yeshiva Gedola Matisyahu
D.N. Modiin 71917 Israel
08-926-1138 Fax 08-926-5326

בס״ד

מ מתתיהו
matityahu

ב׳ דראש חודש

לכבוד הרב

הרב זאב לף
מרא דאתרא מושב מתתיהו
ראש הישיבה ישיבה גדולה מתתיהו
ד.נ. מודיעין 71917
טל. 08926-1138 פקס. 08-926-5326

מושב שיתופי ד.נ. מודיעין 71917 טל: 261016 08 Tel moshav shituti d.n. modiin 71917 israel
פקס: 261124 08 Fax

אור שמח
OHR SOMAYACH

Telephone: (011) 887-1321/2
P.O. Box 646 Highlands North 2037
Fax No. (011) 887-7092

בס"ד ליום ה'

My colleague, Rabbi Avraham Tzvi Schwartz, and member of the Ohr
Somayach Kollel in Johannesburg, has been sharing his "wealth" of
Torah knowledge in our city. He has introduced to many interested
young Jews the beauty and depth of Torah.

Shlomo Hamelech, the wisest of all men expresses the "wealth"
dilemma that confronts man - when he states in Mishlei (30,8)
"Give me neither poverty nor riches, but provide me my allotted
bread."

In his latest book, Rabbi Schwartz has done extensive research to
collect the valuable wisdom of our Torah, in shedding much light on
solving the above dilemma. The reader will find a "wealth" of
knowledge and insights that will certainly enhance his spiritual
growth.

I pray that he will enjoy much success with this book and in all of
his endeavours.

With honour

Yechezkel Auerbach
ROSH YESHIVAH

CONTENTS

PREFACE

A Torah Pursuit?

Is the pursuit of riches, you may ask, not a preoccupation of the secular world? Is it not a secular science? May we make room for it in a Torah library?

We need to remember though, that Torah is all encompassing. One who searches will find that it contains everything – all instructions a person needs to live his life, all wisdom, all understanding. Just as our physical well-being interconnects with our spiritual well-being, so do all the businesses of this world become the Torah's business. The Torah approach[1] is vital to every facet of our lives.

Every person must involve himself in the mundane side of life. He must give it his thoughts and energies. This is his reality. If this then is the case, should he not live his life properly, efficiently, effectively? Should he not study its wisdoms? For he sees that the world is complex, that its businesses are troublesome, and that he easily make mistakes.

The secular sciences claim that they answer the needs of modern man, that they give him the prosperity and well-being he needs. Still, when we look at the world these scientists are building, we notice countless problems – poverty and distress, disharmony and unhappiness. We see a world full of deceit, treachery and the destruction of lives.

The Torah also proclaims that it can cure us of our ailments. First however, we must listen to its words. We must follow its instructions, at the right time, in the right place, and most importantly, with the right attitudes.

From our Rabbis

Our Rabbis strive to show us how to understand and fulfill Hashem's wishes in the best way, and to our best advantage; how to acquire every

---

[1] **The Torah approach...** "When I married," Reb Yisroel Salanter told his students, "I told my wife that I would make the decisions in spiritual matters, while she would rule on those things that affected the material aspects of our lives.

"However, in all our married years, never did we find a question without important spiritual consequences." (Tenuas HaMussar)

prosperity. One who studies their teachings constantly, finds himself delving deeper and deeper into them. As he reviews them, so they become a part of his self, until he burns with a great fire of inspiration and enthusiasm.

When it comes to living in our modern world, we need to scan the Torah and find the answers that bring us to success. The problem though, is that these teachings are scattered throughout the great sea of Torah study. A scholar who swims these seas, may easily stay afloat; he may cling to these magical life-belts and amass great riches. The rest of us however, need help. We need ever-new books to gather in and present to us anew the Rabbis' teachings – to restate them with clarity. This is the purpose of this work.

Here then is a collection of sources gleaned in the main from Tanach, Shas and the Medrash. My main work was to acquire these references, translate them,[2] clarify the points that were most puzzling, and present them to the reader according to subject headings. These preparations however, do not complete the subject. There is much our Rabbis hinted to in their wise words and parables, and the more we probe, the more precious are the treasures we discover. If we will approach the material here with clear heads and a serious attitude, we will find much to enrich our lives.

I am not a master of the gems that this collection contains. Rather, I am a student who, with reference books, has himself discovered these teachings, and then tried, with the help of commentaries and the good sense Hashem grants him, to understand their words. Baruch Hashem I have found much that is interesting and enlightening, many sparkling observations, outlooks, as well as a gold mine of good advice.

It would seem that the best approach to this work is first to read the quotations through, referring only to those notes that clarify the reading. Only then, on the next round, should the reader study the notes with more care. Also, he should note that my footnotes are an incomplete commentary of the teachings. For our Rabbis' words are like a sledgehammer smashing a rock. (Yirmiyahu 23.29) With a few short words, they provide thousands of insights into the workings of the human mind and personality, as well as the world he lives in. While this makes

---

[2] **Translate them** – The rendition here follows a free style; it seeks more to transmit the idea and mood of the verses and teachings, than to accurately translate every word. Since then, this translation is almost a commentary, the inquiring reader should check the teachings at their source.

classifying these teachings under specific headings so difficult, it also, on the other hand, makes the study of such a work, an especial challenge.

May I, together with every reader, merit to review, rethink and meditate on these quotations many times. May we be worthy of uncovering more than a handful of the riches our Rabbis have buried in their nuances and modes of phrase. May we deserve to develop at least a few of the 'seventy faces' of each teaching, and grow great in this knowledge.

I pray now that this work of my hands will provide the reader with much enjoyment and spiritual elevation, and that we, b'ezras Hashem, together with the rest of Klal Yisrael, will learn further, and stride with longer, sturdier paces along the paths of true wealth.

With Gratitude

I offer thanks to the One Whom all thanks belong to. Could I move, could I speak, could I think even one thought, without His help. How much greater then is my debt, now that He has allowed me to finish this work, that He has blessed my efforts with this precious fruit. No word is adequate. No praise is sufficient. All I can hope is that this puny admission of gratitude may somehow, serve as a small thanks-offering.My appreciation of my Maker, however, cannot stop here. There are many who have worked as His agents in developing this book, and I must try humbly, to mention them all. This list also falls short of the praise I owe these holy people. Still, by naming them, I hope that I will in some small way pay my dues.

Those who helped me directly are: Dr. Steven Levy, for his careful proofreading and sound suggestions; R' Shmuel Goldstein and Kevin Kaspar for thoughtfully perusing and adjusting parts of the text; Barak Bar-Chaim, Yerachmiel Moskoff and Danny Kirsh for useful insights, references and advice; Leon Kaplan, Barry Levitt, Neil Levitt, Alan Liknaitzky, Evan Stupel, Danny Shwer, Anthony Awerbuch and Warren Freeman, for patiently hearing me through the sources and ideas of this work; and Yuval Strul, Eitan Schwartz and Steve Weinberg for making my usage of computers and other technology so much easier.

Of those who helped me indirectly, I must mention first, the exciting Kollel program of Ohr Someach, South Africa. It is my privilege to be part of the pilot group, and I have gained greatly by being able to learn and teach within this special kehilla. Thus, I offer my thanks to Mr. and Mrs. Milton Weinberg who power this program with strength and self-sacrifice; Rav Ezriel Tauber who fathered and continues to support the project; Rabbis

Yechezkel Auerbach, Larry Shain, Shmuel Mofson, Zev Kraines and Baruch Goldstuck who infuse the yeshiva with their wisdom and enthusiasm; Messrs. Neil Rubenstein, David Carno, Saul Sackstein, Paul Friedman and their respective families for their generous support; the bocherim of 'The House' for their encouragement; and Lawrence Margolis and the Ohr Someach office staff for their assistance.

In a yet wider sense I add to my list those whose help has set me on the road I follow today. They are the great Torah scholars of early and more recent years, whose teachings pave a highway to approach Hashem with wisdom and love; the yeshivos and their Rabbis who nurture and sustain us with their learnedness and concern; my rebbi, HaRav David Shmidel for guiding me with his vast knowledge; my friends and students who are my partners in discovering truth; HaRav David Sanders and family who continue to inspire me; my in-laws, Reb Moshe Schweber and family for their constant aid; my parents, Mr. and Mrs. Leon Schwartz who deserve the most loving of praises; and finally, my dear wife, Chana, who is my great wealth and treasure-chest of joy.

Also, I honor the reader who gives his precious time to study this work. Just such a kindness enhances this book and gives worth to my efforts. May Hashem bless them all, always!

These then are my thanks to You, Hashem; I know that they are inadequate. My prayer therefore is: "Let the words of my mouth and the thoughts of my heart, please you Hashem, My Rock and Savior." (Tehillim 19.15)

Erev Purim 5757, Kiryat Sefer ת"ו

WEALTH

A TORAH APPROACH

CHAPTER ONE

WHY WEALTH?

Is it Good?

Should we be reading – or writing – Torah books on wealth? Surely it is no more than the pursuit of physical, material acquisitions? And as such, does it not then clash with a Torah life-style? Does it not spoil a person's spirituality?

Still, we find teachings that place wealth in a positive light, just as they scorn poverty. The written tradition itself promises us that when we follow its commands, we will enjoy a plentiful, blessed lifestyle. If wealth then, is something the Torah offers us, surely we should consider it as good?

" ... I will give you rain in its right time, the land will deliver its produce and the trees of the field, their fruit.[1] Your threshing season will extend into the harvest time, and your harvesting will reach into the sowing season; you will eat your food and be content, you will dwell securely in your land, and I will give you peace and harmony ... (VaYikra 26.3-6)

"Hashem will love you and bless you ... He will bless the fruit of your womb,[2] and the fruit of your land, your grain, wine and oil, the young of your herds and flocks..." (Devarim 7.12,13)

"You will be blessed in the city, and you will be blessed in the fields; the fruits of your womb will be blessed ... The fruits of your ground will be blessed and the fruits of your beasts ... Your basket and storeroom will be blessed."[3] (Devarim 28.3-5)

---

[1] **The land will deliver its produce** – Hashem has designed the whole world to produce wealth, and He tells us to 'tap into' this wealth. This is a blessing He bestows on every one of us.

[2] **The fruit of your womb** – Everything in Creation produces wealth. Every element has its usefulness. In some way or another, it serves and thereby, enriches others. Thus every creature adds to the world's fullness.

[3] **Your basket will be blessed** – It is Hashem who creates all things. It is He who allows them to function. Only with Hashem's blessings may they reach their full potential.

Heaven's Glory

We see also how Hashem's prophets praise Him for the wealth and power He owns. Through them, Hashem Himself proclaims that He is Master of all wealth. Would He boast of wealth if it was something lowly and soiled?

"Mine is the silver, mine is the gold,[4] says Hashem, Lord of the Hosts." (Chagai 2.8)

"All in the Heavens and the earth is Yours, Hashem ... all wealth and glory are from You[5] ... You rule over all." (Divrei haYamim 1.29)

Self Esteem

A person with wealth, stands up. His wealth gives him a sense of confidence that allows him to act, a sense of self-worth that fills him with enthusiasm. He enjoys all that he is and all that he does. He feels important and this promotes his success. Thus his wealth is a key to prosperity – a key that opens the doors to his desires.

"The ground under their feet" (Devarim 11.6). This verse, taught R' Elazar, refers to a person's wealth – it stands him on his feet. (Pesachim 119a)

Rav Shmuel bar Nachman said: When a man is wealthy, he shows his friend a happy face.[6] (Breishis Raba 91.5)

R' Elazar said: A man who has no land is no man.[7] (Yevamos 63a)

A beautiful home expands a person's thoughts. (Brochos 57b)

Beautiful garments enlarge a person's thoughts. (ibid.)

The rich man's wealth is his fortress.[8] (Mishle 10.15)

---

[4] **Mine is the gold** – People are naturally possessive. They hold tightly onto that which is theirs. However, their ownership is limited. While they may enjoy their possessions as long as they are alive, eventually they must let go. The only true owner is Hashem.

[5] **All wealth and glory are from You** – Even that which a person does gain in this world, he only gains from the One who is the ultimate Master of all.

[6] **A happy face** – When a person feels good about who he is, he finds it easy to show a happy face. This however, is only possible when he appreciates the wealth he has.

[7] **He is no man** – To conquer and acquire is an intrinsic quality of man's personality. Without satisfying such a need, he cannot actualize his 'manliness.' (R' Lewis Furman, shlita)

[8] **His fortress** – It removes his fears, replacing them with confidence.

The rich man has many who love him. (Mishle 14.20)

Wealth adds many friends.[9] (Mishle 19.4)

Healthy Wealth

There is wealth to be had; there is money in the streets. However, a person needs to want this money, to look carefully for it, and gather it up. For the Heavens guide a person in the way he wishes to go (Makkos 10b). True, there are hardships he must endure; he must learn to toil; he must train himself to wait, patiently. Still, if he wants it, it is there. The question is though, should he want wealth?

At the simplest level we may answer that the survival of religious life depends on wealth. We need money for our Shabbosim and for our weekdays, for talleisim and for tefillin. We need money for our shuls and our schools. We need money to create libraries and feed our scholars. The very survival of a Torah life-style depends on a financial backing. To raise whole families, a nation who lives with true values, all requires successful economics. Thus every aspect of the Torah depends on wealth.

R' Elazar ben Azarya would say: If there is no flour, there can be no Torah. (Avos 3.21)

Food leads to laughter, wine adds joy to life, and money solves all problems. (Koheles 10.19)

Poverty's Curse

Over and above this, our Rabbis point to the serious handicaps that poverty creates.

Throughout this work there are numerous references to Shlomo haMelech's great works: Mishle, Koheles and Shir haShirim. If we are careful to study and contemplate them, we will profit well; for he is particularly well qualified to teach us about wealth. Besides being the wisest of men, he was also one of the richest men who ever lived. Our Rabbis tell us that he was so wealthy that he made gold as plentiful in Yerushalayim, as stones. (Orchos Tzaddikim, introduction)

[9] **Many friends** – This speaks of one who is rich in both wisdom and physical possessions. For not only do deceitful people attach themselves to the rich man; rather, even sincere, good people are attracted to him. They look to him as a model of success, and are eager to be his friends and students.

At a deeper level this teaching hints to those who are rich in Torah wisdom. They are the ones who merit true friends. (Vilna Gaon)

The poor man's wisdom is ridiculed; no one listens to his words.[10] (Koheles 9.16)

The poor man's brothers hate him, even his friends keep their distance; they call him a hound.[11] (Mishle 19.7)

The poor man is hated even by his friend. [12] (Mishle 14.20)

Rav Shmuel bar Nachman said: When a man is poor, he cannot show his face [13] to his friends – he is ashamed. (Breishis Raba 91.5)

A poor man abandons his friend.[14] (Mishle 19.4)

Four are considered as though they were dead; *a pauper*, a *metzora*,[15] a blind man and one who has no children. One who knows such people,[16] should pray for them. (Nedarim 64b. Tosephos there)

The Rabbis taught: Three things lead to insanity and heresy. These are (1) contact with idolaters, (2) an evil spirit and (3) *extreme poverty* ... [17]

---

[10] **No one listens to his words** – "If all his wisdom has not brought him success," a person thinks, "can it then have any worth?!"

[11] **A hound** – They feel unable to improve his fortune and are therefore uncomfortable in his presence. He is a source of embarrassment. Even when he does not beg them for help, they feel threatened by his poverty. They sidestep him, as they sidestep a mulish dog.

[12] **Even by his friend** – Even when the pauper has a very special friend, he ultimately loses him. For to keep the friendship alive he must reciprocate in some way; and without this reciprocation, the relationship will die.

[13] **He cannot show his face** – Poverty may have certain good features, but where it stops a person from being his true self, where it withholds him from living a full life, we must call it bad. Where it prevents him from relating normally with others, and even kills his smile, it is evil. Every person must rid himself of such a poverty. This is essential.

[14] **Abandons his friend** – We understand why the pauper's friends avoid him, but why should he abandon them? This however, is his sad plight. Since he feels that they resent him, he does not ask for their assistance, even in situations where they would be glad to help him.

[15] **A metzora** – One afflicted with a spiritual disease that resembles leprosy. One who is a metzora must often live in isolation; a pain as great as death.

[16] **One who knows such people** – All four types speak of those who are unable in some way, to give to others. The pauper has nothing to give; the metzora is isolated from others; the blind man is helpless; and the childless person has no child who depends on him. The inability to give is one of the greatest losses of all. It is a loss so great that our Rabbis equate it with death. (Sichos Mussar 32.31)

Obviously though, if any of these four types is able to learn, devise or find ways to give of themselves to others, they free themselves of this death.

One who knows such people, should pray for them. (Eiruvim 41b)

The Rabbis taught: There are three types whose lives are no lives:[18] (1) he who hopes to the tables of others; (2) he whose wife rules over him; (3) he who is afflicted by bodily pains. Others teach that there is a fourth type – he who has only one shirt. (Beitza 32b)

R' Yochanan and R' Elazar both said, "When one becomes dependent on others, his face becomes like a *krum*. What is *krum*? Rav Dimi stated, " ... this is a bird that lives by the sea; when the sun shines it changes to a number of colors."[19] (Brochos 6b)

Rav Ami and Rav Assi stated: "One who depends on others is like a man condemned to a double punishment – water[20] and fire."[21] (Brochos 6b)

---

[17] **Extreme poverty** – To maintain his mental health, a person must live a normal life – and "normal" to a large extent means that he eats certain foods, wears certain clothes, lives in a certain house, etc. All this helps him to think good, positive thoughts. Conversely, extreme poverty obstructs a person from all this, and thus induces insanity.

Moreover, one who is extremely poor lives with the feeling that Hashem doesn't care for him. Thus he may reject Hashem as Master of all. A second, deeper reason is that a person naturally senses the existence of a Divine force and a heavenly glory. We see this clearly in small children. Unless they live in an environment that forces heretic thoughts on them, they are happy to have Hashem in their lives. However, extreme poverty and other forms of abnormal living may lead a person to insanity, and thereby to denying Hashem.

[18] **Whose lives are no lives** – There are different elements a person needs to feel 'alive.' They include feelings of security, self-esteem, well-being, and according to others, a sense of space. The four types listed above each represent one of these needs: For (1) he who hopes to others' tables, lacks a sense of security; (2) he whose wife rules him, is deprived of self-respect; (3) he who is afflicted by bodily pains, lacks a sense of well-being; while (4) he who has only one shirt lives under pressure – he does not enjoy the space, that expansive feeling that accompanies prosperity. All these deficiencies deaden his life.

[19] **A number of colors** – Man is a noble being. He contains inherent greatness. Thus when he must lower himself, he suffers much embarrassment. This causes his face to change color.

Such shame may however, also be a gift. It pushes a person to strive constantly for added achievements, for new heights. However, when he is lazy and slothful, he eventually loses this sense of embarrassment. He learns in his laziness, to rely only on others and loses all feelings of shame.

[20] **Water** – Water, in its negative context, symbolizes lust (Shaar HaKedusha). A person who follows his lusts, is a very lowly person. Like water, he creeps into all

R' Pinchas ben Chama taught: Poverty in a man's house is worse than fifty lashes.[22] (Bava Basra 116a)

R' Avahu taught: There is no suffering in the world as severe as poverty ...

"What would you prefer," Hashem asked Iyov (Job), "poverty or afflictions?"

"Lord of the universe," Iyov answered, "give me all the sufferings in the world, but not poverty. Help me that I need not walk down the street without a coin in my hand – without the money I need to buy a little food. (Shmos Raba 31.12)

Our Rabbis taught: If all the world's sufferings sat on one side of the scale, and poverty on the other, it would outweigh them all. (Shmos Raba 31.14)

The pauper's poverty[23] brings to his ruin. (Mishle 10.15)

Reish Lakish taught: When a person becomes poor below, he becomes poor Above.[24] (Sanhedrin 103b)

---

types of unsightly places. To silence his cravings, he becomes a complete slave to his desires. Thus his lusts rob him of all self-control and 'drown' him.

When a person must depend on others, he too becomes helpless; he too suffers from a lack of control. This is the punishment of "water."

[21] **Fire** – Fire in its negative context, represents arrogance (Shaar HaKedusha). Similarly, the punishment for arrogance is fire. As the person elevates himself over others, leaping above them like a flame, so he condemns himself to a burning shame. His haughtiness leads him from one embarrassment to the next.

One who begs for help – unless he is a complete fool – must also lower his head. He too suffers the fires of shame.

[22] **Fifty lashes** – The number fifty symbolically represents 'the world'. One who suffers extreme poverty is like one who has lost his entire world.

[23] **The pauper's poverty** – What is the pauper's poverty? Is there a poor poverty and a rich poverty? The answer is yes! When a man rich in good qualities tastes poverty, this stirs him to action. While he may be depressed at first, he soon rebels against this state. He strives to change it. Thus his poverty challenges him to reach new heights. However, when poverty challenges a man poor in good qualities, he is crushed.

[24] **He becomes poor Above** – A person does not lose his wealth without a good reason. Should his fortunes fall, while others around him prosper?! We must therefore say, that he is to blame. His has not behaved in a way that matches his true nobility. This in turn, has sickened his attitudes and attributes. With his ugly actions and unpleasant ways, he has distanced himself from others, and no one wishes to help him anymore. Moreover, his loss is a double one – for the very

Poverty's Benefits

There is however, also a very positive and good side to poverty; a side that makes all this suffering well worth while.

Eliyahu haNavi once said to Ben Hei-Hei, (and some say to R' Elazar), "What does the verse, 'I have purified you, but not with money, says Hashem, rather I have selected you in the crucible of poverty'?[25] (Yishayahu 48.10)

"It teaches," he continued, "that Hashem sorted through all the good attributes, but found none as good as poverty."[26]

Shmuel (and some say Rav Yosef), said, "This fits the folk-saying: Poverty is as beautiful for the Jewish people as a red strap on a white horse.[27] (Chagiga 9b)

Good Living

Poverty encourages a certain lifestyle, and this is a lifestyle that has some definite advantages; advantages such as living with foresight, unity and a joy of life.

Why do we call matza the 'bread of poverty'?

---

factors that bring him to poverty in this world, also impoverish him in the world-to-come.

[25] **The crucible of poverty** – Refineries smelt gold at extremely high temperatures, thus separating the pure gold from the dross. In a same way, Hashem subjects his beloved to the excruciating pains of poverty; He wishes them to reach ever-higher levels of purity.

[26] **None as good as poverty** – Wealth allows a person the freedom to do many things. It frees him from the curse of poverty. He is able to pursue that which is aesthetic and beautiful. He can afford to be charitable and altruistic. Thus his riches may buy him new levels of piety.

Still, when Hashem wishes the Jewish people to reach higher levels of refinement, he does not do this with riches. He has a far more effective tool – this is poverty.

[27] **A red strap on a white horse** – Seeing a white horse in a dream, is a good omen. (Brochos 56b) This is because the color white indicates that we are whitened of our sins. Red on the other hand, indicates the opposite; moreover it points to the harsh decrees that come in the wake of our sins. Thus the red strap on the white horse represents how poverty, although it is cruel, brings us to a purer, cleaner state.

A further thought: Just as a white horse is beautiful, needing no more than a red strap to emphasize his glory; so Torah study and observance, while it may involve difficulties, beautifies Yisrael. They need no gold and silver to highlight their splendor; their lifestyle alone adorns them. (Maharsha)

One explanation is that just as the poor man breaks his bread in half, eats one half and keeps the other, so we have the custom to break the *mitzva matza* in half.

Another explanation is that just as the poor man fires the oven while his wife bakes, [for they can't afford to fuel the oven for too long], so we bake the *matza* with great haste.[28] (Pesachim 116a)

Rav Assi said: Why are the festivals so happy in Babylon? – Because they are poor.[29] (Shabbos 145b)

Spiritual Gains

Moreover, in a person's spiritual growth, poverty functions as an especially valuable tool.

During times of trouble the congregation should appoint a wise man, accustomed to leading the prayers, who has children to feed and an empty house – so that he may pray with a full heart.[30] (Taanis 15a)

R' Yitzchak said: [Of the flour-offering] Hashem says, "Who is it that brings Me a flour-offering – the pauper?! I will count it as though he offers *his life!* (Menachos 104b)

Keep an eye on the poor – for from them will emerge the next generation's scholars.[31] (Nedarim 81a)

---

[28] **Bread of poverty** – This teaches two of poverty's good qualities. One is that just as the wise man looks into the future (Tamid 32a), so the strain of poverty also forces a person to peer into and plan his future; it forces him to ration his food, keeping some for later. Thus, his poverty steers him away from laziness, training him to work and save. The second quality is that a poor person must cooperate and team up with others, in order to make the most of his lot.

Both the qualities of living carefully and working with others are positive, and lead to healthy living, to happier, fuller lives. A wealthy person however, with all his independence, may never learn these attributes. He may never come to experience these very rich aspects of life.

[29] **Because they are poor** – All year round they have no rest from their labors, and so they cannot enjoy their food and drink; they are only free to enjoy the fruits of their labors during the holidays. Thus their holidays give them a special joy. (Rashi)

[30] **That he may pray with a full heart** – A person reaches a peak of closeness to Hashem when he is most under pressure. This is especially so when he suffers from poverty. It is then that he realizes how feeble he is, and how much he depends on Hashem. Thus, his poverty brings him to a new bond and love of his Maker.

R' Avahu taught: Hashem tests the pauper: Will he will accept his sufferings without ranting and raving? ... If he passes this test, Hashem doubles his reward in the world-to-come.[32] (Shmos Raba 31.3)

When a pauper sins, Hashem does not blame him for this, for he is not thinking as he should.[33] (Zohar Chodosh, Acherei 49)

"He releases the poor man through his poverty" (Iyov 36.15) – this teaches that Heaven frees those who suffer poverty from the punishment of *Gehinom*.[34] (Yevamos 102b)

Three groups of people are exempt from even seeing *Gehinom*; these are those who suffer from (1) extreme poverty, (2) stomach pains and (3) debts.[35] Others add, those who suffer from wicked wives. (Eiruvim 41b)

---

[31] **The next generation's scholars** – This is a command to all Torah teachers: Do not treat the poor lightly. Do not withhold from teaching them. For from amongst them will come the Torah leaders of the next generation. (Rashi)

Why especially the poor? – Since they are not distracted by other occupations and interest, and also since they are humble, they study with a seriousness that leads them to greatness. (Ran)

[32] **Hashem doubles his reward** – Will he despite his hardships, recognize Hashem's goodness? Will he thank Hashem for his kindness and compassion? If he passes this test, he reaches a very high level; he becomes twice the person.

[33] **He is not thinking** – As we learnt above, poverty brings to insanity. There is a back-handed benefit here. This is that poverty frees the person from liabilities and duties that others must pay for.

[34] **They are released from** Gehinom – As terrible as poverty is, it is still small change compared to Gehinom; as our Rabbis teach, the fires of Gehinom are one sixtieth of the fires in this world (Brochos 57b). A moment of suffering in Gehinom may in effect be more terrible than a life-time of the Iyov's suffering. Surely it pays to suffer a little poverty to escape this horror?!

Why should poverty release a person from Gehinom? For it prompts a person to exchange his evil ways for better ones. The lessons he learns from poverty save him from such a hell. Still, our Rabbis teach, there is another option. If a person will serve Hashem with awe, he also escapes the torments of Gehinom. Thus the same Gemara teaches further:

"The angel of Hashem encamps around those who fear Hashem." (Tehillim 34) – this teaches that the reward for those who fear Hashem, is that they are released from Gehinom. (Yevamos 102b)

Which is the lesser price to pay, poverty or the awe of Hashem? The answer should be obvious.

[35] **Debts** – This accords with Rashi's translation. According to Tosephos however, it refers to one who is hounded by the police.

Hashem tested out all attributes and found none as good for Yisrael as poverty;

- through poverty, they fear Hashem,
- through poverty, they do charity,[36]
- through poverty, they do acts of kindness,
- through poverty, they learn Torah.[37] (Tana d'Bei Eliyahu Zuta 5)

When Hashem will come to save Yisrael, who of Yisrael will be the first to enjoy His mercies – the poor.[38] (Shmos Raba 31.12)

One who is poor in this world, is wealthy in the world-to-come.[39] (Osios d'R' Akiva, Dales)

A Fool's Wealth

There is a clear distinction between the money we need to sustain and support ourselves, and the wealth that buys us more than our immediate needs. Normally, we think of wealth as something beyond food and shelter, something richer than tables and beds, than lights and water.[40] Instead, we think of power and prestige, of luxuries and respect. We think of dignity and honor. Is such an honor something we need?

Our Torah tradition teaches us that wealth is the pursuit of fools. Furthermore, we see that our Rabbis point out the very real benefits that

---

[36] **They do charity** – Only one who tastes poverty can know how much it hurts. This hurt, in turn, stirs him to help others. For if he feels compassion, can he hold back his help?!

[37] **They learn Torah** – This is the only precious commodity a person can acquire for himself, without paying a large sum of money.

It follows then, that since Hashem only sends us poverty to teach us to be charitable, learn Torah, etc., we may well avoid it by learning these lessons ourselves. Moreover, if we follow Hashem's wishes well enough, we may even push poverty from our lives, forever.

[38] **First to enjoy His mercies** – For they are humble.

[39] **Wealthy in the world-to-come** – The sufferings of poverty alone, besides the spiritual levels he reaches, enrich him in the next world.

[40] **Something more than food and shelter...**

"Bless my son that he will be rich," the father asked the saintly Rabbi.

"Riches?! Peh! Who needs riches?!" the Rabbi exclaimed.

"But how then will he live?" his worried father asked.

"Oh, you're asking about livelihood," the Rabbi said, "that's something else completely. May Hashem grant him his livelihood, in abundance!! (Heard from Rav Shmuel Yitzchok Herman, zt"l)

poverty brings to. Should we then desire wealth and avoid poverty? Should we read books that speak of acquiring riches?

"A wise man's heart turns to the right..." (Koheles 10.2) these are the righteous, who give their hearts to acquiring Torah.

"...a fool's heart[41] turns to the left,"[42] (ibid.) these are the wicked, who put their heart into becoming rich. (BaMidbar Raba 22.9)

The rich man must use his wealth to buy his life,[43] but the poor man is not threatened. (Mishle 13.8)

With more wealth, come more expenses – what pleasure then does its owner enjoy, other than to see it?[44] (Koheles 5.10)

There are wealthy men who earn money, amass fortunes, but die without children; their moneys enter the king's treasuries.[45] What does the king do with this wealth? He builds public utilities for the benefit of the poor. (Shmos Raba 31.11)

Yet despite money's harmful nature, most people cannot get enough of it...

He who loves money, is never satisfied with money. (Koheles 5.9)

---

[41] **A fool's heart** – A fool is one who loses that which you give him. (Chagiga 4a) Accordingly, one who puts all his energies into becoming rich, is also a fool. He forgets and thereby, forfeits the spiritual side of life, and with it, his world-to-come.

[42] **To the left** – The right indicates a person's good inclination, while the left represents his evil inclination. Every person has both such inclinations. A wise person, however, understands that he only enjoys true prosperity when he directs his attentions towards that which is right!

[43] **To buy his life** – The rich face greater dangers than the poor. They fear for their wealth, and even their lives. Therefore they must invest much money into protecting themselves. Still, worse than the cost of this protection, is the nagging worry that threatens their health and sense of well-being.

[44] **Other than to see it** – There are ultimately few pleasures the rich man enjoys beyond his poor neighbor. Even his added prestige soon disappears. For as he moves up the social ladder, he again associates with people who are not impressed by his wealth.

[45] **The king's treasuries** – Just as no person wants to die, so he doesn't want his hard-earned wealth to die. This however, is exactly what happens to wealth. It passes on to other hands, and disappears.

Is it good then?

Why did they call R' Menachem b'Rebbi Simai, child of the holy? Because he never even looked at a coin.[46] (Avodah Zoro 50a)

Do not weary yourself to become rich, leave off your plotting.[47] (Mishle 23.4)

Heaven's Blessings

There are definitely advantages a pauper enjoys, both in this world and the next. However, there is a good type of wealth too; a wealth that helps a person grow spiritually. Still, this is not the wealth that the wicked pursue, a wealth that must be snatched; rather it is a wealth that comes with Heaven's blessing. It is a gift from Hashem. As such, it contains the potential to raise a person to elevated heights.

> Hashem created three gifts in this world. If a person merits even one of them, he merits the world's delight. If he merits wisdom, he merits all. If he merits might, he merits all. If he merits wealth,[48] he merits all. (BaMidbar Raba 22.7)

When does one who merits such gifts, merit all?

> This is when they are Heaven's gifts; gifts that come from the Torah's power; however the might and wealth of flesh and blood, are nothing. (ibid.)

> The verse says: "Hashem's blessing makes a person rich, *without* adding to his worries."[49] (Mishle 10.22)

---

[46] He **never even looked at a coin** – The biographers of the saintly Chazon Ish tells us that after touching money, he would wash his hands. He strove to detach himself from the materialism of this world, and reach instead, ever-higher levels of purity.

[47] **Do not weary yourself** – If one strives only to acquire more and more money, he misses out on the true richness of life. He forfeits that which is pleasant and helpful. Ultimately, such living is unhealthy and harmful. (Vilna Gaon)

[48] **If he merits wealth** – The wealth the Torah admires, is a special type of wealth, a heavenly wealth; one that comes as a gift from Hashem. However, 'man-made' wealth is of small of value, and may even lead to a person's downfall.

[49] **Without adding to his worries** – Even though it says "One who increases his property, increases his worries" (Avos 2.7), still when his wealth comes from Hashem, it comes without toil and worry. Where Hashem sends His blessing, there one may dwell serenely. (Vilna Gaon).

Any person to whom Hashem has given wealth and property, allowing him to eat of it, take his share, and rejoice in his labors, has received Hashem's gift. (Koheles 5.18)

It is the gift of Hashem that a person may eat, drink and see the good of all his labor. (Koheles 3.13)

When the years prosper, people treat each other like brothers[50] ... there is love and friendship in the world. (Breishis Raba 89.4)

One who has never tasted Jewish money, is like one who has never tasted bread.[51] (Shocher Tov, Tehillim 14)

For His Glory

Wealth plays a special role in a Torah life. There is an importance it possesses that goes beyond life's basics, or even its luxuries and comforts. This is the influence that wealth has on us as a people, and the world around us in turn.

The ideal the Jewish nation strives for is to teach ourselves first, and then others, how to serve Hashem. As a people who live according to such an ideal, we need to display the success-formula this ideal contains. We must represent to all how Hashem blesses our lifestyle with all types of prosperity. We must display to others the great worth of keeping the Torah's commands. This is logical.

The Torah personality who is also wealthy, is one of the best teachers. His happiness and the heavenly blessing he enjoys, spill over and encourage others to live a Torah life. His wealth stirs others to fulfill Hashem's every wish. This is especially true for those who best live up to the Torah ideal – the righteous and the wise.

The crown of the wise[52] is their wealth ... (Mishle 14.24)

---

[50] **Like brothers** – Their prosperity affords them a generosity of spirit and an affection for all men.

[51] **One who has never tasted bread** – This refers to wealth that belongs to those Jews who keep mitzvos and are close to Hashem. For the closer they are to Hashem, the more the Heavens bless their wealth. Such money tastes like no other money in the world.

[52] **The crown of the wise** – A wise man who has wealth is respected. Thus it is a crown for him. This however, is not the case with the fool. His wealth is a source of scoffing; people only squeeze him for as much as they can. Thereafter, they are quick to disregard and discard him. (Vilna Gaon)

R' Shimon ben Menasia quoted in the name of R' Shimon bar Yochai: Beauty, power, *wealth*,[53] honor ... are good for the righteous, and good for the world. (Avos 6.8)

R' Shimon bar Yochai once noted that a friend of his, a very wealthy man, was living on lentils.

"Could it be," he asked him, "that a man as wealthy as you, feeds his family such cheap food?"

"Rebbi," the man answered, "It's easy for you to talk – people honor you for your great Torah scholarship; but if we will squander our wealth, who then will honor us?!" (Esther Raba 2.4)

---

[53] **Beauty, power, wealth** – These are qualities that all people admire. When they notice that it is the righteous who merit these fine features, they learn to follow in their righteous ways.

CHAPTER TWO
HEAVENLY WAYS

Where is It?

The first thing a person should realize is that any success, financial or otherwise, is not in his hands. Every person needs Heaven's blessing, and he must climb certain steps to merit it. Even then, despite his efforts, his success is not guaranteed.

Shlomo haMelech says: "I have contemplated and seen under the sun,[1] that it is not the swift who win the race; nor the mighty who triumph at war; it is not the clever who have bread, nor the insightful who have wealth, nor the knowledgeable who are liked – for the ruins of time and circumstance come on them all." (Koheles 9.11)

Surely man walks in darkness; surely he strives in vain – for he heaps up riches, but does not know who will gather them in.[2] (Tehillim 39.7)

Heavenly Acts

The coming of Moshiach, the rebuilding of the Holy Temple, the in-gathering of the exiles from the furthest corners of the earth, the recognition of the world that Hashem is One, and that the Jewish people are his agents, are all goals beyond human grasp. All these goals depend on supernatural intervention, Hashem's miracles. Our Rabbis teach, however, that just as this final redemption depends on Hashem, so too does a person's livelihood.

R' Eliezer taught: The Torah compares *Geula* to earning a living,[3] and earning a living to the *Geula* ... Just as the *Geula* is most wondrous, so too, is earning one's living a wondrous phenomenon ...

---

[1] **Under the sun** – The term 'under the sun' is used many times in Koheles. It refers to this physical world. This is the world that is under the sun, as opposed to the world of the spirit, which is beyond the sun.

[2] **Who will gather them in** – He doesn't know whether he will enjoy them, or whether someone else will.

[3] **The Torah compares Geula to earning a living** – Another feature common to Geula and one's livelihood is that we receive both of them every day! Just as

R' Shmuel bar Nachman said: Earning a living is greater than the *Geula*, for the *Geula* comes by way of an angel, while one's livelihood comes directly from Hashem ...

R' Yehoshua taught: Earning a living is greater even than splitting the Yam Suf (the Red Sea).[4] (Breishis Raba 20.22)

In His Hands

R' Yochanan taught: There are three keys Hashem does not give over to any intermediary, but rather holds in His hands. These are the key of the rain, the key of giving birth, and the key for resurrecting the dead ...

"Surely," the *Gemara* asks, "the key of sustenance[5] is also in Hashem's hand?"

"Rain" R' Yochanan would respond, "is sustenance." (Taanis 2b)

R' Eliezer ben Yakov said: When the rains descend, they bring blessings to one's business dealings. (Devarim Raba 7.6)

Rav Yitzchak said: Great is the day that it rains – for rains bring blessings even to the penny in ones pocket.[6] (Taanis 8b)

"How long did it take Hashem to create the world?" A Roman noblewoman asked R' Shimon ben Chalafta.

"Six days," he answered.

"And since then what is He doing?"

"He sits and makes ladders," R' Shimon told her, "lowering one person, and elevating another."[7] (BaMidbar Raba 22.8)

Heaven performs marvelous miracles each day to feed us, likewise it performs marvelous miracles each day to bring us the Geula. Why then do we not enjoy the Geula yet? – We must say that it is our shallow habits and selfish ways that prevent it from flowering.

[4] **Greater even than splitting the Yam Suf** – Hashem even violates the rules of nature to provide a person with his living. Just as to split the sea Hashem had to change the world, so He breaks His own rules to feed us.

[5] **The key of sustenance** – One reason why Hashem controls our livelihood directly, is that we may realize that it is He who feeds us. He wants us to appreciate in ever-deeper ways how He supervises all, that we may thereby come closer to Him.

[6] **Rains bring blessings even to one's pocket** – Rain is not only the symbol of life; it is also the symbol of wealth. Thus the word geshem (rain) is the same as the word gashmius (material wealth). While the rain itself only affects fields and orchards, still there is a Divine blessing that descends with it, that permeates everything.

"Hashem makes low, Hashem makes high," He takes this one's money,[8] and gives it to that one. This is why property is called nechasim, Hashem covers it (mechaseh) from one, and reveals it to another.

Similarly – currency is called *zuzim*, for they move *(zazim)* from one person to the next.

Likewise, money is called mamon or maneh, for one does not know whether that which he counts *(moneh)* has any worth – it may shortly belong to another!

It is also called ma'os; for it is only temporarily *(ma-eis)* in your possession. (BaMidbar Raba 22.8)

Early Beginnings

Heaven determines the fortunes of the individual. It is with such a fortune that each person begins his life.

R' Chanina bar Papa taught: The angel appointed over pregnancy is called *Leila*; and he takes the droplet before Hashem and asks, "What will be with this droplet? Will it be strong or weak? Will it be wise or foolish? Will it be wealthy or poor?" The only question he does not ask is, "Will it be righteous or wicked?" For as R' Chanina taught, all is in the hands of Heaven except for the awe of Heaven.[9] (Nida 16b)

---

[7] **A Roman noblewoman** – The Romans were at one time, the world's rulers. In their own eyes they were masters of all civilization and culture. Certainly every pleasure and luxury was theirs? Certainly the world was theirs, and all should bow to them? What then, could Hashem's role be?!

Rebbi Shimon hinted to this 'noble' woman that Hashem had not relinquished His ownership; and that He may even deprive her of all her wealth and pride. Just as Hashem sends food and other forms of prosperity to the world as a whole, so too He determines each individual's prosperity. He constantly adjusts and readjusts a person's fortunes.

[8] **He takes this one's money** – Naturally, the mightiest should win all the world's treasures, the fiercest, most ambitious should capture and enjoy all pleasures. However, Hashem does not allow this 'survival of the fittest' rule to control people's fortunes and fates. Rather, His Divine Justice intervenes even in this element of our lives.

[9] **The awe of Heaven** – It is in this respect, and this respect alone, that a person has full free choice.

R' Akiva said: A father bequeaths[10] to his child his beauty, strength, *wealth,* wisdom and life-span. (Adios 2.9)

Divine Decrees

Every day a heavenly voice announces:[11] "So-and-so's daughter goes to So-and-so. So-and-so's wife goes to So-and-so. So-and-so's money goes to So-and-so. And some say that it also announces, So-and so's house goes to So-and-so." (Kala Rabsi 8)

R' Elazar ben Pedas was extremely poor. Once, he was feeling very weak and had nothing to eat. He found a garlic sprout and ate it. This however, made him still weaker, and he dozed off ...

Later he related the following dream: "Hashem was sitting with me, and I asked Him, "How long must I suffer in this world?"

"Elazar, My son," He told me, "would you prefer Me to dissolve the world, and begin it again? Maybe then you will be born in a time when food is plentiful."

"You would go to so much effort for me," I asked, "and still, only *maybe* my lot will improve!" I then asked Him: "Have I lived most of my life already, or not?"

"You have lived most of your life," He answered.

"If so, I don't want You to dissolve the world."[12]

---

[10] **A father bequeaths** – Yet another way the Heavens influence a person's fortunes, is when they choose his parents for him.

The Rambam comments that generally, a child inherits his parent's physical attributes and character traits. These in turn, determine his wisdom, prosperity, etc. Also, the father who is wise, trains his child how to acquire wisdom; while the father who is wealthy in turn, teaches his son how to advance his wealth.

[11] **Every day a heavenly voice announces** – While Hashem sets a person's life right from the start, His influence does not stop here. At later stages of his life He adjusts his fortune. He evaluates his daily affairs in relation to his spiritual standing, and adjusts it according to His greater world plan. Then He allocates and reallocates to him a whole range of resources.

[12] **If so, I don't want you to dissolve the world** – We see here that Hashem 'desired' to enrich Rebbi Elazar, but was 'unable' to do so. Still, ultimately all is just. While Rebbi Elazar suffered in this world, Hashem compensated him fully, in the next world. Just for refusing Hashem's offer to start the world all over, he received a magnificent prize.

Still this teaching is most difficult. Why should Hashem be unable to enrich Rebbi Elazar? Is there something Hashem cannot do?!

"As a reward for this," Hashem then told me, "I am giving you thirteen rivers of pure saffron oil in the world-to-come..."" (Taanis 25a)

Do not say: So-and-so is rich, and I am not rich; not everyone merits to sit at two tables.[13] (Derech Eretz Zuta 4)

Mazal

In general, the influence coming down from Heaven follows set paths. Each path brings for different people different levels of success and prosperity. Thus, a person who is on the 'right path' at the right time, may receive a large measure of such wealth, while another person, one whose influence follows a different path, will need to make do with less. We commonly refer to these paths as a person's fortune, or mazal.

Certain people are set on paths of wealth. This is their lot by heavenly decree. This doesn't always mean that they will be wealthy; but it shows that wealth is something very much within their grasp. If they want it, it's theirs.

Can we identify such paths? One view holds that it is the day of his birth that determines one's mazal. Another says that it is the hour of the day that makes the difference.

There are two major points that explain this. One is that the world must go through certain phases before it may reach its special goals. An example of such a phase is an era where great tzaddikim live in absolute poverty and deprivation.

A second point is that while all souls have the potential to reach great spiritual heights, only a few of them do so. These are the souls of the tzaddikim. Therefore, because there are so few of them, Hashem has 'to spread them finely throughout the generations.' (Yoma 38b)

So while all depends on Hashem's desire – and He may easily will a person to be rich, wise or strong – still the ways of Heaven are not so simple. Sometimes Hashem's 'hands are tied.' Because of the many, great calculations Hashem makes that the world may reach its final destination, Hashem must decree poverty on certain tzaddikim. Which then of these precious souls will fulfill the special role of living in poverty? – For this, Hashem 'draws lots.'

[13] **Not everyone merits two tables** – It is common practice to judge people according to their material wealth. This however, is a mistake. The person who is richer or poorer than his friend, is not necessarily greater or lesser than him. Likewise, he is not necessarily more or less righteous. Two people may have identical merits, yet still enjoy different fortunes.

In R' Yehoshua ben Levi's notebook it was written: One born on the third day (Tuesday), will be wealthy and immoral.[14] Why? For on this day, Hashem created the grasses. (Shabbos 156a)

Rav Chanina taught: It is not the day that determines one's fortune, but the hour ... thus, one born when the star "Noga" shines will be wealthy and immoral. Why? For this is the moment Hashem created fire.[15] (ibid.)

Ten measures of wisdom came into the world; *Eretz Yisrael* took nine of them, and the rest of the world took one.

Ten measures of beauty came into the world; Yerushalayim took nine of them, and the rest of the world took one.

Ten measures of wealth came into the world; the early Romans took nine of them, and the rest of the world took one.[16]

---

[14] **Wealthy and immoral** – Grasses have two attributes. One, they flourish richly. This is an omen that one born on the third day will flourish and prosper, similarly to grasses. However, they also have a second characteristic – they intermingle with each other. This indicates that one born on the third day has an inclination towards immorality. To receive his world-to-come, he will have to resist and overcome the temptations of immorality. (Rashi)

Likewise, we learn here that wealth and immorality are inter-linked. The reason is that wealth and 'wealthy living' attracts immorality. This is a serious drawback for one who seeks wealth. He must take care that his losses do not outweigh his gains.

[15] **Hashem created fire** – Fire, with proper control, brings much benefit – warmth, energy and light. However, it is also a destructive force. It has a strength and power to consume anything flammable.

Wealth, like fire, is also a force. It gives a person access to all types of power and pleasure. Thus "Noga", the heavenly source of fire, points to great potential wealth. However, it also points to the problems that come with wealth, namely, the indolence and lusts that accompany such a life-style – attributes that may well rob a person of all his spirituality.

[16] **Ten measures of wealth** – Just as Hashem determines the fortune of the individual, how wise, powerful and rich he will be, so too He determines the fortunes of each nation. (Maharsha)

Different nations have different strengths and weaknesses. This potential allows them to succeed or fail as they reach for their material and spiritual objectives. Thus, while a person may become wise anywhere in the world, the potential for wisdom is nine times greater in Eretz Yisrael. Similarly, while he may become wealthy anywhere in the world, the potential to acquire great wealth is nine times greater in ancient Rome. Who is today's successor to ancient Rome? – Possibly, what we call the Western World.

Ten measures of poverty came into the world; Babylon took nine of them, and the rest of the world took one.[17] (Kidushin 49b)

The Dispute over Mazal

Is mazal (fortune) something that affects all people equally? There are views that mazal holds no sway over Yisrael. Instead, they teach that everything depends on a person's merits and his service to Hashem.[18] Still, other views differ.

Rava said: A person's life-span, his children and his wealth do not depend on merit, rather all depends on his *mazal*; as we see with Raba and Rav Chisda. Both were great, righteous men, yet when the one prayed, rain would fall,[19] while when the other prayed, rain would not fall. (Moed Katan 28a)

R' Chanina taught: One's *mazal* enriches and one's *mazal* impoverishes. *Mazal* plays a part in the lives of Yisrael. (ibid.)

R' Yochanan says: *Mazal* plays no part in the lives of Yisrael. (Shabbos 156a)

Rav Yehuda said in the name of Rav: When *Avraham Avinu* told Hashem that the stars indicated that he would have no children, Hashem answered him: "Leave your star-gazing,[20] there is no *mazal* for *Yisrael*"[21] (ibid.)

What we learn then is that a person may succeed to a greater extent in one place as opposed to another – whether in regard to acquiring wealth, or wisdom.

[17] **Ten measures of poverty** – Poverty is not just the absence of wealth, but rather itself, a distinct attribute. Therefore, when the Gemara states that Babylon received nine portions of poverty, it actually received something! This fits the idea that Hashem's influence penetrates every element of the world. Even that which the world lacks, is a creation of Hashem.

[18] **His service to Hashem** – One person's service may require that he has great wealth. His wealth is the 'tool-set' he needs to fulfill his mission. In contrast, another person may only be hampered by such wealth, and to accomplish his task he needs poverty.

[19] **Rain would fall** – Rain is linked directly and indirectly with food, prosperity and blessing.

[20] **Leave your star-gazing** – Avraham saw that according to his mazal he could not have children.

"This doesn't worry Me," Hashem told him, "and it shouldn't worry you either. Your mode of living is above the stars. They have no control over your life."

[21] **There is no *mazal* for** Yisrael – In truth, there is no dispute between these views. While we say that Yisrael is affected by mazal, a person who has extraordinary

Dreams

The Heavens may at times inform a person that his fortune is changing. One way they may do so is through dreams.

> The Rabbis taught: If one sees Rebbi in a dream,[22] he may hope for wisdom; if he sees R' Elazar ben Azarya[23] in a dream, he may hope for wealth. (Brochos 57b)

---

merits may live beyond his mazal. His service of Hashem alone brings him all the success he desires. At other times however, mazal overrules a person's prayers and merits. It alone determines the workings of his everyday. It decides his successes and failures. (Tosephos)

When a person is on a high spiritual level, when he builds a special relationship with Hashem, then Hashem personally supervises his life. But, when he distances himself from Hashem, Hashem too 'turns His back' on him, and leaves his fortune in the hands of the stars. Thus, to move beyond one's mazal, a person must move closer to Hashem.

[22] **Rebbi in a dream** – There are different reasons why a person may dream of wise and wealthy personalities. One is that a higher dimension of his conscience knows of future occurrences in his life, and informs him of them through his dreams. This accords with the teaching that dreams are a sixtieth of prophecy (Brochos 57b). Accordingly, dreams may certainly point to future wealth or poverty.

A second reason however, is as our Rabbis teach, that that which a person dreams of at night, reflects that which he thinks about during the day (Brochos 56a). A person dreams of certain personalities because he has been focusing on these persons. He has imprinted their images on his sub-conscience. This seemingly robs dreams of their importance. "If they are only the product of my thoughts, and not prophecy," a person may complain, "surely they have no worth?!"

However, even such dreams may indicate future prosperity. They may be more than just "leftover thoughts." For when a person thinks of great people, this shows that he is trying to emulate their successes; it indicates that he too, strives for greatness. He is a man with a vision, and as such he will achieve and accomplish. His thoughts permeate his actions, and his actions in turn, determine his success. Thus his dreams lead him to glorious goals.

Unfortunately though, this section on dreams applies less to us today. We are so accustomed to distractions and so unaccustomed to thinking, that we know little more than the mumble-jumble of our fast lives. Thus, our dreams are little more than a confusion of fleeting images.

[23] **Rebbi ... R' Elazar Ben Azarya ...** – While Rebbi was also one of the richest men of his time, still his greatness and wealth of learning overshadowed his financial splendors. On the other hand, Rebbi Elazar ben Azarya, although he was also a great sage and was even appointed to head the Sanhedrin, stood out amongst his fellow-Rabbis specifically because of his wealth.

"If one sees a snake[24] in a dream," a student recited before Rav Sheishes, "his livelihood is assured; if it bites him, it is doubled; but if he kills it, he loses it."

If he kills it," Rav Sheishes told him, "all the more so it is doubled."

This however, is not so,[25] says the Gemara, Rav Sheishes only said this because he had killed a snake[26] in a dream. (Brochos 57a)

Other Signs

Rav Yitzchak taught: A year that is poor at its start, is rich at its end.[27] (Rosh HaShana 16b)

----

[24] **If one sees a snake** – The snake is a symbol of a person's evil inclination. Every living person must fight against and try conquer this force. Should he however, ignore it, he will certainly not succeed.

The person who sees the snake is a person who knows that he has a battle to fight. Thus, he lives his life for the very reason Hashem gave it to him, and merits thereby, still more life. Hashem assures him of his livelihood. Moreover, if he sees the snake biting him, this is an even better sign. It means that he sees how fierce his battle is – how it is a fight for his spiritual life, or death.

On the other hand, when he sees himself killing the snake, this may indicate that the battle is over, as is his reason for living. Hence, his living allowance has also ended. Once he lays down his arms, he must leave this world.

[25] **This however, is not so** – Rav Sheishes argued that since the snake represents a person's evil inclination, it is the evil of his life. Therefore, when he kills it, he surely merits life's blessings. Should this not then entitle him to a generous livelihood? However, since this world is only a corridor for the world-to-come (Avos 4.21), which means that we are here only to fight our evil inclinations, the Gemara rejects Rav Sheishes' interpretation.

[26] **He had killed a snake** – A rule regarding dreams is that they follow their interpretation. Thus, even if someone has a negative dream, he may interpret it in a positive way. The reason for this is that the dream, before it enters reality, exists as a raw force in a non-physical realm. Thus, it can be drawn down in a number of ways, both negative and positive. (Shiurei Daas vol. 1, p.108)

Rav Sheishes therefore, wished to interpret his own dream differently, thereby rendering it harmless. For although he was a righteous man, one who had done much to kill 'the snake', he still wanted to live.

[27] **Is rich at its end** – Likewise, at the beginning of a new venture, a person begins 'a new year.' His start is a new era in his development. Here too, he should know that 'all beginnings are difficult.' (Mechilta, Yisro 19) Once he learns all he needs to learn, and suffers all he needs to suffer, he may yet merit that Hashem will save him. While he suffers hardships at first, he may yet trust that his situation will improve.

One who begins a business and wishes to know if it will succeed or not, should breed a chicken. If it grows fat, he may know that he will succeed.[28] (Horios 12a)

Another important lesson here is that when Yisrael 'impoverish' themselves at Rosh haShana, the New Year, beseeching Hashem like paupers who have nothing to eat, then they merit a rich year. (Rashi)

[28] **He will succeed** – One reason for this is that if his mazal is good, then it will fatten his chicken; while if his mazal is poor, the chicken will suffer. Another reason is that the taste of success in a small project, will give him confidence. The lesson here then, is that a person should first try a small venture, before he tackles a grander scheme.

CHAPTER THREE

WORKING

A Special Blessing

While one's *mazal* may entitle a person to wealth, still it does not exempt him from making his own efforts and exerting himself. On the contrary, even good *mazal* may require special input before its owner realizes his fortune. Also, a person by exerting himself may change his *mazal*. A change of residence or name already changes his *mazal*. (*Rosh haShana 16b*) How much more is this so when, through his own efforts, he changes himself! This is part of the special blessing that comes from hard work ...

> Greater is the merit of ones own labors, than the merit of the *forefathers*. (Tanchuma, VaYeitzei 13)

> Rebbi Chiya bar Abba said in the name of Ulla: Greater is one who enjoys the labor of his own hands,[1] than one who regards Hashem with awe

---

[1] **Greater is one who enjoys the labor of his own hands** – When one labors himself, he reaches a clearer recognition that the source of wealth is only Hashem. Daily he sees that while he toils on one project, his income comes from another source. With his every venture he has an opportunity to learn that it is Hashem who enriches him, and not the work of his own hands. Thus, he is greater than the one who, while regarding Hashem with awe, cannot reach this understanding. (*Rav Chaim Shmulewitz z"l, Sichos Mussar 31.20*)

A broader explanation of the above teaching goes as follows: One who lives only from his *Yiras Shamayim*, who relies on his reputation as a holy man to support him, eats from the rewards of his world-to-come. Thus while he may live well in this world, ultimately, he will suffer for this. When he sees how his table in the next world lacks that which he consumed here, he will be bitterly hurt and ashamed. On the other hand, one who toils in this world, eats from the fruit of his own labors, and not from his ultimate reward. (*Maharsha*)

But, we may ask, surely the *Kohanim* of old, as happens with many Torah scholars today, were supported by the community? Surely they received financial assistance *explicitly* that they may serve Hashem?

We may understand this as follows: A person who serves the community by performing a religious function, or if he is a scholar, by enriching the generation's Torah knowledge, fulfills a role no less than a president or a prime-minister, a policeman or a street-cleaner. Just as such civil servants require suitable wages, so

(*Yiras Shamayim*). While he who regards Hashem with awe is fortunate in this world ... he who toils, enjoys this world, and also delights in the goodness of the world-to-come. (Brochos 8a)

Better is the person who lacks honor, but has a servant,[2] than the refined man who has no bread. (Mishle 12.9)

Must We?

Hashem created the world with kindness; He did not put people in this world that they might suffer. Still all around us, we see much distress. How can this be?

The answer is in the verse, *"Man was born to toil"* (Iyov 5.7). When a person works hard and thinks hard, converting his conclusions to action and effort, he fulfills his task in the world. For Hashem created him to toil, and this is what he is doing. Moreover, Hashem in turn, rewards him by filling his many needs.

However, when a person avoids working hard, when he refuses to think before acting, Heaven deprives him of his needs. This causes him to suffer, which is another type of 'toil.' The Heavens substitute the trouble and pain he avoids by not working, with external trouble and pain. If he will not *afflict himself*, problems and worries from the outside world will pursue him.

Thus we see that hard work is one of the best antidotes to suffering.

"With the sweat of your brow you shall eat bread." (Breishis 3.19)

Rebbi Avahu taught: While the upper ones, the angels and other celestial beings, are nourished by the sheen of the Divine Presence; lower beings,

---

should those who help the community fulfill its religious duties, receive generous salaries. No one will begrudge them such payment. However, insofar as such a person takes from others *without offering a service in return*, he will indeed find that his table in the next world is lacking. For instead of taking funds from his heavenly *expense* allowance, he has drawn instead, on his heavenly rewards.

[2] **A servant** – Who is the person who lacks honor, yet has a servant? It is the person who is prepared to be a servant to himself, i.e., to accept even lowly work for his livelihood. He is far better off than the refined man who will not engage in menial labor, and starves. (*Rashi*)

From here we learn that one who is willing and eager to undertake any type of task, is like *the man who has his own slave*.

those who live in this world, *must toil*[3] – if they don't, they don't eat! (Breishis Raba 2.2)

To the man who says, "I will eat, drink and enjoy all that's good *without toiling*, for I trust that Heaven will take mercy on me," the Rabbis say, you are wrong!" The verse expressly states that, "*You [Hashem] bless the deeds of his hands.*" (Iyov 1.10)

A person needs first to labor[4] and work with his two hands, only then does Hashem send His blessing. (Tanchuma, VeYeitzei 13)

Only with Toil

The effort a person must make is vital. Even though his livelihood comes from Hashem, he must give his whole self, heart and all, to his labors. Otherwise, his efforts will produce very poor fruits.

Rav Assi taught: Earning one's livelihood is twice as hard[5] as bearing a child. (Breishis Raba 20.9)

Wealth that comes without toil,[6] diminishes; but he who gathers in gradually, constantly, increases his wealth. (Mishle 13.11)

One who works his land, will be satisfied with food. (Mishle 12.11)

There is much produce with the strength of the ox.[7] (Mishle 14.4)

---

[3] **Lower beings must toil** – Even if a person is the greatest *tzaddik*, and lives with the utmost trust in Hashem, still he is obligated to toil.

[4] **A person needs first to labor** – Every person must work. If he wishes to live a good, healthy life, he must toil. The effortless path does not exist, and if a person persists in searching for it, he will end up only with *Gehinom.*

[5] **Twice as hard** – After Adam and his wife sinned, they were both punished. Adam was told that "with the sweat of your brow, you will eat bread" *(Breishis 3.19)* while Chava (Eve) was told, that she would "bear children with grief and pain" *(ibid.).* Of the two, Adam's curse was the harsher one.

One reason for this is that the essential hardship a man suffers is the worry, the torturous thought that accompanies one who has responsibilities. This itself adds a great weight to the toil he must suffer. *(Yefei So'ar)*

[6] **Wealth that comes without toil** – With labor, a person's efforts produce healthy, constant fruit. Without labor, it is a case of easy come, easy go. *(Vilna Gaon)*

[7] **The strength of the ox** – It is not the ox itself that produces food, but rather the *strength* of the ox that does so – the toil, effort and continuous push of doing a little bit more. Similarly, it is a person's toil and effort, and not his natural talents, that bring him to riches.

Rebbi Yehoshua ben Levi said: Today is *for doing*, tomorrow is not *for doing* ...

Today is *for doing*, tomorrow *is for receiving reward*.[8] (Eiruvim 22a)

Whatever your hand can do, *do* – with all your strength – for there is no deed, calculating, knowledge, or wisdom in the pit you travel to. (Koheles 9.10)

Ben Hei-Hei said: According to the pain[9] is the reward. (Pirkei Avos 5.23)

Trading

What occupation then should a person choose? While our Rabbis teach that the person who works should do so with all his strength, this does not mean that a person must work physically. Buying and selling[10] of goods is also work, and as we learn here, may be a very profitable pursuit.

Rava said: Invest a hundred zuz in business, and you eat meat and wine everyday; invest a hundred zuz in ground, and you eat salt and hay; moreover you sleep on the ground.[11] (Yevamos 63a)

Rav Yitzchak said: A person should always have ready cash, [that when a bargain comes his way, he may buy it[12] – *Rashi*]. (Baba Metzia 42a)

---

[8] **Tomorrow** – While tomorrow here refers to the next world, a world where the righteous bask in the golden sheen of the Divine Presence, it also refers to the tomorrow of our every day. The Rabbis warn us here not to push off the obligations of today to another day.

[9] **According to the pain** – This is Hashem's golden rule; you get what you pay for. We must note also, that 'toil' means more than straining ones physical muscles. A person must use his other faculties too. Moreover, the greatest successes come when a person employs *every* talent he has. This is especially true when he dedicates the excellence of his thought to prayer and Torah study.

[10] **Buying and selling** – See Rebbi Yehoshua's teaching on the connection between business and prayer on p.152.

[11] **You sleep on the ground** – for he needs to watch his property constantly that no one steals its fruits. *(Rashi)*

What may we learn from Rava's teaching? What is it that makes business better than farming? One thought is that farming entails investing much money and energy into a piece of land, i.e., property of a permanent nature. Business on the other hand, is flexible, and often even portable. Thus, since we live in a passing, temporary world, business is the activity that more readily matches the world's make-up and spiritual thrust. For this reason it succeeds more readily.

[12] **He may buy it** – When a person is employed by others, he leaves little room for Hashem to enrich him. His salary is already set, and there is no place for Hashem's

All who occupy themselves in building,[13] become poor. (Sota 11a)

... and Trades

However, a person should only choose 'business,' if he has some talent in this field. If not, he may just starve, or worse, he may steal.

What does the pauper know about property and business?

What then should he do, sit idly? Rather, let him learn a trade,[14] and Hashem will sustain him. (Koheles Raba 6.8)

The Rabbis taught: One is obligated to teach his son a trade.

Rebbi Yehuda taught: Anyone who doesn't teach his son a trade, teaches him to be a robber. (Kidushin 29a)

"How does Rebbi Yehuda's view differ from the Rabbis'?" asks the *Gemara*, "surely they say the same thing?"

"The Rabbis understand," the *Gemara* answers, "that one who teaches his son to do business, also fulfills his obligation, whereas Rebbi Yehuda holds that this is not sufficient. His son may not succeed in business, and

---

blessing to take effect. However, when he works for himself, the field is more open. There are 101 areas through which Hashem may send his blessing, if he will only find a little favor in Hashem's eyes. *(The Skverer Rebbi; heard from Rabbi Eliezer Medwed, shlita)*

[13] **All who occupy themselves in building** – Building seemingly, is a relatively straightforward trade; surely a person can rake in fine profits here. However, it requires a lot more experience and expertise than even an intelligent person would first assume; and without this a person is heading for trouble.

The *Pele Yo'etz* writes: In general a person is able to calculate how much new acquisitions will cost him and then check his purse to see if he can afford it. In this way, he avoids poverty. This however, is not the case with building. What he thinks will cost him a hundred, ends up costing two hundred. Also, once he starts building, he cannot retract. Thus he impoverishes himself. Therefore, if a person wishes to build, he should first calculate if he can pay twice as much as he originally estimated. If he can, then he may build; if not, let him worry first about his store. As people say: The store builds the house (i.e., buying and selling brings profits), but the house does not build up the store.

[14] **Let him learn a trade** – Certain people are miserable failures when it comes to doing business. Still success does await them. There is a great rule that if a person does that which he knows how to do, that which his natural inclination leads him to do, he will succeed. Hashem implants in him a potential to follow just such a route – and when he strives to reach it, Hashem will reward him with success.

without a trade to fall back on, he may resort to theft.[15] (Kidushin 30b and *Rashi* there)

Occupations

For work to conform with a Torah life-style, there are certain rules a person must follow. Likewise, for work to succeed practically, there are certain rules he must follow. If we study the teachings of our Rabbis, we will see that these two sets of rules, are really *the same* – the very rules that fit into a Torah life-style, are the rules that lead to practical success.

The most important of these rules is *to know* that while a person must plan and labor intelligently, ultimately his success comes only from Hashem. He must recognize that (1) it is really Hashem who supports him, and (2) it doesn't really matter which occupation he chooses. If he has the merit and the *mazal*, Hashem will support him generously.

> Rebbi Meir said: A person should always teach his son an occupation that is clean[16] and easy,[17] and pray to the One who owns all wealth and possessions;[18] for a person's occupation affects neither his poverty nor his wealth, rather all depends on one's merit.[19] (Kidushin 82a)

Or according to a different version ...

---

[15] **He may resort to theft** – The Torah's ruling however, follows the Rabbis' view that when a person teaches his child to do business, he fulfills his duty.

[16] **Clean** – A person should pick not only that which is physically clean, but also that is spiritually clean – there should be no element of dishonesty or theft mixed-in with it.

[17] **Easy** – This means that it should not involve huge capital outlays and expenditures – neither financial, nor physical. (*Tosephos Yom-Tov*)

A person only picks an occupation that is difficult or messy, because he imagines that he will earn greater rewards. Still such reasoning is faulty – his livelihood comes only from Hashem. And while it is true that he must toil, he may still choose a clean and easy occupation. Moreover, a clean and easy craft will leave him with time and energy to learn Torah and fulfill *mitzvos* in an optimum way.

[18] **And pray to the One who owns all wealth** – While, in general a person's prosperity is decided by his *mazal*, there are times when a person's merits may change his *mazal*. Then there are times where only very extraordinary merits will override his *mazal*. And finally, there are instances where even such merits cannot undo his *mazal*. At such a time a person should turn to prayer. (*Tosephos Yom Tov*)

Still, we should know that ultimately Hashem is fair and executes His justice with precision. Each person will receive the rewards and punishments he deserves, whether in this world, or the next.

[19] **All depends on one's merit** – including his prayers.

Rebbi Meir said: A person should always teach his son an occupation that is clean and easy, and pray to the One who owns all wealth and possessions; for a person's occupation affects neither his poverty nor his wealth, rather *all* depends on He who owns all wealth, as the verse says, *"Mine is the silver, and mine is the gold, says Hashem, Lord of the Hosts."* *(Chagai 2.8)* (Kidushin 82b)

A person should therefore, seek out the most pleasant occupation.

Rebbi said: The world cannot be without a perfumer, nor without a tanner; fortunate is the one whose trade is making perfume; woe to the one whose trade is tanning.[20] (Kidushin 82a)

Don't Worry

A person should not be afraid to pursue the profession that really appeals to him. Hashem can feed him just as well, no matter the path he chooses.

Rebbi said: There is no trade that disappears from the world[21] ... (Kidushin 82a)

In *all* toil there is profit. (Mishle 14.23)

---

[20] **Making perfume...tanning** – When a person's work is making perfume, he is surrounded with pleasantness; at work the scent surrounds him on all sides, after hours it clings to him even as he goes home. The tanning process on the other hand, involves working with smelly dog-droppings. The stench of this occupation likewise, becomes a part of his reality. Wherever he goes and whatever he does, it imprints itself into his entirety.

In the non-physical sense too, a person's work affects his personality. There are crafts that fill a person with joy and even elation, while other occupations crush and depress him. For this reason our Rabbis advise us to look for occupations that are pleasant.

Sometimes however, Heaven arranges it that a person enters a profession that is difficult and unpleasant. For special reasons they force him into a certain job. If this is a person's lot and he cannot avoid it, he must learn to accept it with joy. He should focus on the thought that Hashem only does that which is best for him, and accordingly, this too is for his benefit. Still, where he can avoid such an occupation, he should do so.

[21] **There is no trade that disappears from the world** – and so a person should not worry that his choice may become outdated and obsolete. The idea here is that while we do see such a phenomenon – machines and technology replacing people – still Hashem does not abandon any person. The training and preparation he invested into learning one trade will serve him just as well, if not better, in the occupation he eventually does practice. Just as Hashem guided him through his training, so Hashem guides him throughout his working life.

Those who sow with tears, reap with joy.[22] (Tehillim 126.5)

He who walks, crying, carrying the bag of seeds, returns in joy, carrying his sheaves.[23] (Tehillim 126.6)

Hashem does not withhold the reward of *anyone* – no matter the field a person toils in, he produces heavenly rewards; as the verse says, *"He who plants the fig tree,*[24] *eats its fruit."* *(Mishle 27.18)* (Tanchuma, Naso 13)

---

[22] **Reap with joy** – On the other hand however, those who sow with joy, i.e., they do not toil sufficiently and treat their work with disdain, end up *reaping in tears*. *(Chafetz Chaim)*

[23] **Carrying his sheaves** – The act of 'carrying' which at first, was so uncomfortable, so painful, *itself* becomes a source of great happiness. As he carried in pain, so he will carry in joy.

[24] **He who plants the fig tree** – A further idea here is that the fig tree produces figs, while a poison ivy produces poison. Similarly, the occupation a person chooses determines its fruits. When a person engages in good, wholesome activities, he may expect to eat good, wholesome fruits. However, when he busies himself in deceitful, wicked activities, he will ultimately eat bitter, venomous foods.

CHAPTER FOUR
ON YOUR WAY

Be Wise

The first of wisdom[1] is "get wisdom." (Mishle 4.7) It is better to acquire wisdom than gold.[2] (Mishle 16.16)

The best of gains is gaining insight. (Mishle 4.7) To gain insight is preferable to silver. (Mishle 16.16)

If you are wise, you are wise for yourself ...[3] (Mishle 9.12)

He that gains wisdom loves himself; he that advances his understanding finds goodness. (Mishle 19.8)

Wisdom provides protection, and money provides protection; but the advantage of wisdom is that it is a source of life for its owner. (Koheles 7.12)

Wisdom is better than strength. (Koheles 9.16)

There is gold, large pearls and expensive vessels[4] in knowing lips.[5] (Mishle 20.15)

---

[1] **The first of wisdom** – Before a person learns wisdom, he should aspire to wisdom. This means that (1) he should appreciate its greatness, its importance; and (2) he should desire it greatly. He should hunger for it so, that he learns it from all people (Avos 4.1), at all times, in all situations – and with enthusiasm. Only then may he hope to acquire it, and enjoy a full success.

[2] **Better than gold** – The gold a person spends helps him but once, but his wisdom helps him again and again.

[3] **You are wise for yourself** – While learning Torah wisdom is Hashem's command, still He gives us this mitzva for our benefit. It is we who profit from following His instructions!

[4] **Gold, large pearls and expensive vessels** – Each element here represents a different type of wealth. Gold is buying power; large pearls (pearls of great worth) are hoarded wealth; while expensive vessels are items that serve the person in the best possible way, bringing comfort to his life. All these belong to the person who acquires knowledge. (Vilna Gaon)

[5] **Knowing lips** – Greater than the wise man is the wise man who teaches and enriches others. He uses his power of speech to help others towards success; and this in turn, furthers his own accomplishment.

Rav Zutra bar Tuvia said in the name of Rav: Hashem created the world with ten elements;[6] with *wisdom, understanding, knowledge,*[7] power, discipline, might, justice, law, kindness and mercy. (Chagiga 12a)

With wisdom a house is built, with insight it is readied, and with knowledge its rooms are filled with precious, pleasant wealth. (Mishle 24.3,4)

One who acquires wisdom, acquires all. (BaMidbar Raba 22)

R' Yitzchak said: One who wants to be wise, should turn [when he prays] to the South; one who wants to be wealthy, should turn to the North.[8]

R' Yehoshua ben Levi taught: Always turn to the South, for if you are wise, then you will be wealthy. (Bava Basra 35b)

Luxury does not befit a fool.[9] (Mishle 19.10)

Worldly Advice

No person may succeed in isolation. He must have the help of others. An area where this is especially important is in seeking good, proper advice.

Salvation comes with much advice.[10] (Mishle 11.14)

Without advice even a nation tumbles. (ibid.)

---

[6] **With ten elements** – These are the basic elements of all Creation.

[7] **Wisdom, understanding, knowledge** – Dr. Gerald Schroeder, a prominent physicist, has stated that just as man understands how all matter comes only from energy, so he may one day understand how energy comes from wisdom. (Heard by the author)

The lesson here is that if Hashem needs wisdom to build this world, certainly then, puny man needs wisdom to build up his personal world. Thus, the first rule to prosperity and every achievement is 'GET WISE.'

[8] **South ... North ...** – On the South side of the temple stood the menora, the symbol of illumination and wisdom. Thus, the person who turns to it, shows that this is what he wants. His action points to his desires. Such action speaks louder than words.

On the North side of the temple stood the golden table laden with its twelve special bread-loaves. It is the symbol of wealth. The person who turns himself towards this, turns towards wealth.

[9] **A fool** – On the contrary, it destroys him. And who is the biggest fool? – The person who follows his lust for luxuries, allowing them to intoxicate and spoil him.

[10] **With much advice –** A person wishing to enter a certain field must make sure that first he gathers all necessary information. If he wishes to avoid great and expensive mistakes, he needs loads and loads of advice; he must listen, and listen, and listen.

Open your eyes,[11] and you will be satisfied with bread.[12] (Mishle 20.13)

Don't sign sureties[13] you cannot pay for. Why should they take your bed from beneath you? (from Mishle 22.26)

The Torah teaches us the ways of the world – a person should not put all his money in one corner.

Who do we learn this from? – from Yakov, as the verse says, "and Yakov divided his camp." (Breishis 32.8) (Breishis Raba 76.3)

Rav Yitzchak said: A person should divide his wealth three ways,[14] a third he should invest in land, a third in stocks and a third in cash. (Bava Metzia 42a)

A person should sell his fields to buy flocks;[15] he should however, never sell his flocks to buy fields. (Chulin 84a)

"It's bad, it's bad," sighs the buyer [as he examines the goods,] but when he departs, he gloats.[16] (Mishle 20.14)

---

[11] **Open your eyes** – Opportunities surround us on all sides; but a person has to open his eyes and see them. This too, is a part of the required effort. This too, is a necessary tool of success. He must pocket his pride, and learn to seek the advice of others.

[12] **With bread** – Stores sell bread and they sell straw. Thus, the person who is lazy and does not make a proper effort to acquire goods that are good, ends up with the inferior product – even as he pays the full price! (Vilna Gaon)

[13] **Don't sign sureties** – One who signs as a guarantor for others, should be ready to pay their debts. If not, he should not sign.

[14] **Three ways** – Rav Elchonan Wasserman zt'l remarks that we see from this teaching how the Torah penetrates and illuminates every element of our lives, even our finances. It is the true source of advice and salvation. (Ikvesa d'Meshicha) This is clearly stated in the verse: "Mine is the advice and salvation," says Hashem. (Mishle 8.14)

A person should remember though, that the Torah's ideas often go beyond logic. Therefore, to take full advantage of its wisdom, he should first probe the idea with his own intellect, as well as with the advice of trusted friends, and then listen to the Torah's words. Only thus may he hope to understand its directions, and merit a full salvation.

[15] **Sell his fields to buy flocks** – One who has flocks, has milk to drink and wool to make clothing. (Rashi)

We learn here that only if a person has what to eat and what to wear, may he then invest in fields. In other words, a person must first ensure that he has a livelihood, the resources he needs to feed and clothe his family. Then may he worry about long-term investments.

[16] **It's bad, it's bad** – Therefore be careful not to lower your price too quickly!

Management Checks

R' Yitzchak taught: Better off is one who has his own garden,[17] fertilizing, hoeing it and living from the proceeds, than one who works many gardens for half the profits. As people say: He who operates a single garden eats birds, whereas he who operates many gardens, birds eat him. (VaYikra Raba 3.1)

Be tireless to know the welfare of your flocks, and attend well to your herds,[18] for riches do not last forever. (Mishle 27.23,24)

Setbacks

Faith too plays a part in being wise. A person must know how to suffer setbacks, and still thank Hashem for his lot. He must believe that all Hashem does is for his benefit.

There were two men who set out on a business venture. One of them stepped on a thorn, and was unable to continue. He began to curse his bad fortune. However, after a few days, he heard that the ship he missed had drowned. He then began to praise and thank Hashem. (Nida 31a)

Not Enough

Still wisdom by itself, does not guarantee everything. A person may be wise and not succeed.

---

[17] **Better off is one who has his own garden** – Even if a person doesn't own a garden, and hires one, he profits more than the person who contracts to work many gardens, but cannot do so properly. The one who works a single garden well, eats birds; he enjoys the fruits of his toil and lives a good, pleasant life. However, the one who is grasping, taking on more than he can manage, chokes in his greed, and in the end, the birds pick at his bones. The message here is that modesty in business brings to profits, while greed for big profits leads to collapse. (Matnos Kehuna)

Alternatively: One who has a single garden is able to guard it from the birds. Moreover, when they come, he catches and eats them. However, when he has many gardens, he cannot guard them properly, and the birds eat the fruits of his labor. (Rav Zev Wolf Einhorn)

[18] **Be tireless to know** – Check on them yourself, and do not rely on others to do this for you. (Malbim). **Attend well to your herds** – that they reproduce as they should. **For riches do not last forever** – While wealth flows into your pockets today, it does not promise to return tomorrow. (Vilna Gaon)

Raban Gamliel once asked R' Yehoshua: You have so much wisdom, yet you sail [on business to earn your livelihood?]

"Instead of being amazed at me," R' Yehoshua answered, "be amazed at two of your own students ... they know how to calculate how many drops of water the sea holds, yet they have neither bread to eat, nor garment to wear!"[19] (Horios 10a)

Wisdom is good with an inheritance.[20] (Koheles 7.11)

Good Attributes

Wisdom also teaches a person the necessity of good attributes and how they may bring him riches. Still, if the person does not work to acquire them, he has no more than a nice set of ideas. He must exert maximum effort to pursue good traits and avoid negative ones.

The first of good attributes is a willingness to work quickly and whole-heartedly ...

The hand of the diligent enriches. (Mishle 10.4)

The hand of the industrious rules;[21] the lazy man, however, must follow instructions. (Mishle 12.24)

The quick worker is richly endowed. (Mishle 13.4)

Did you see the man who works quickly;[22] he will stand before kings. (Mishle 22)

───────────────

[19] **Neither bread to eat** – As Shlomo haMelech says: It is not the clever who has bread, nor the insightful who has wealth. (Koheles 9.11)

[20] **With an inheritance** – This inheritance refers to the spiritual merits one receives from his fathers, both his immediate ancestors, as well as the holy forefathers. (Rashi) Also, it refers to wealth or a skill one receives from his fathers. (Sforno) The good start that an inheritance gives a person, gives his wisdom something to work with.

We learn here that a person should not discard or belittle anything that his fathers give him. If our Rabbis tell us that wisdom is good with an inheritance, then a person should incorporate this in his bid for success.

[21] **The hand of the industrious rules** – He is the one who receives positions of authority and responsibility. The lazy man, however, remains in a lowly position all his life.

[22] **The man who works quickly** – The habit of working seriously is an attribute that brings to wealth. Another attribute is the ability to work quickly and continuously, without laziness or procrastination.

Powerful men attain wealth. (Mishle 11.16)

The wealth a diligent man accumulates is precious. (Mishle 12.27. Rashi there)

He that works his land will have much bread. (Mishle 12.11)

On the other hand ...

Idleness leads to hunger (Mishle 19.15)

A slack palm brings to poverty. (Mishle 10.4)

How long will you sleep, you lazy one? When will you arise from your rest? A little sleep, a little slumber, a little folding of the arms to rest – and your poverty comes marching in. (Mishle 6.9-11)

Do not love sleep; it will impoverish you. (Mishle 20.13)

Laziness brings a person to deep sleep. (Mishle 19.15)

The lazy man lusts in vain. (Mishle 13.4)

The lazy man's desires kill him,[23] for his hands refuse to work. (Mishle 21.25)

He who is slack in his work, is a brother to *the destroyer*.[24] (Mishle 18.9)

Ambitions

While ambition, the desire to always acquire more, is often a negative force, a wise person uses it in a positive way. He harnesses his hunger to produce healthful fruits – a wealth that brings him closer to Hashem. Thus he reaches greater and greater excellence. Also, since his hunger serves as a silent prayer to Hashem, Hashem helps him achieve his dream.

The laborer's hunger labors for him; his mouth's desire pushes him to do more.[25] (Mishle 16.26)

The man who gets the job done, is the man everyone seeks. Many people are able to begin a project. Greatness, however, lies in taking it to its completion.

[23] **The lazy man's desires kill him** – It takes only a word or even a thought to arouse a desire. However, to do and achieve something requires physical effort. Since the lazy man's hands refuse to do his wishes, he remains with his desires alone – desires that only frustrate, and ultimately, even kill him.

[24] **A brother to the destroyer** – The lazy man who does not mend that which decays and breaks, is in effect, destroying his world.

[25] **His mouth's desire** – The mouth that eats, is a symbol of man's continuous appetite and desire to gain and consume more.

While in the morning you sow your seed, do not rest in the evening from your labors, for you do not know which will prosper – these or those, or possibly, even both. (Koheles 11.6)

You open Your hand [Hashem] and satisfy every living being with *his desire*.[26] (Tehillim 145.16)

He satisfies the soul that pangs; He fills the hungry with goodness. (Tehillim 107.9)

Grabbing

While ambition may be positive, snatching and grabbing are definitely negative traits, and lead only to losses.

He who chases after riches,[27] will not remain clean [of sin]. (Mishle 28.20)

The mean man rushes to acquire wealth – little does he know that he will come out with less.[28] (Mishle 28.22)

A greedy heart creates only controversy, while he who trusts in Hashem will be sated with riches. (Mishle 28.25)

This is the way of the person greedy for gain – his pursuit of it robs him of his life. (Mishle 1.19. Rashi, Ibn Ezra there)

Patience

Patience is one of the most important of all attributes. A person must learn to wait, and not 'force the moment'. Hashem owns all, and all comes from Him. A person should therefore, ready himself to wait for Heaven's gifts.

One who adds to his wealth little by little,[29] eventually has much. (Mishle 13.11)

---

[26] **His desire** – Hashem gives the person the very thing he desires. (Metzudos Dovid) If he will only desire it truly, Hashem will make it his. This is a great principle of Torah thinking. An amazing power lies in every person's hands. By harnessing his ambitions correctly, he may receive his every wish. Still, he must be careful to desire only that which is good. That which is evil will bring him to evil.

[27] **He who chases after riches** – He tries to force Hashem to give him wealth, and this leads him to oppress the poor. (Rashi)

[28] **The mean man** – In his greed, he steals that part of his income that he should have given to charity. Such a person however, only ends up poorer; for he places a curse on his own wealth. (Rashi)

[29] **Little by little** – While his contributions may be small, still there is a cumulative effect. His constant, consistent effort brings him a special blessing. If he will only

Rav Ada bar Ahava saw a non-Jewish woman wearing a *karbalto* (an expensive, provocative garment). He thought she was Jewish, and ripped it off [in protest at her immodesty]. He then discovered that she was not Jewish, and that he was obligated to redress her embarrassment with a payment of four hundred *zuz*.

"What is your name?" he asked her.

"Mitun," she told him. [This name in Hebrew means 'patience'.]

"Mitun, Mitun," he said, "you cost me four hundred *zuz*."[30] (Brochos 20a)

The spoken word leads to loss.[31] (Mishle 14.23)

Tolerance

Another important attribute that helps a person profit, as well as live a long, pleasant and happy life, is tolerance.

The Torah instructs a person to easily forgive the monetary losses his family creates at home.

The wine spilt? Forgive them,[32] says Hashem, for I replenish the righteous.

---

wait – without despairing or diminishing his labors – he will eventually reach every success.

[30] **Four hundred zuz** – Had Rav Ada bar Ahava displayed a little patience before acting, he would have saved himself four hundred zuz.

The word mitun is also related to the word matayim which means 'two hundred.' Just as twice two hundred is four hundred, so does a double dose of patience save a person much money, and even help him to profit.

[31] **The spoken word** – There is no organ in the body as quick to work as the mouth. Moreover, it produces its words at an amazing pace, speaking as much as 200 words per minute. (Chafetz Chaim, Shmiras haLashon) Thus a person must exercise a special patience and caution before he allows it 'to shoot.' Also, many situations call for silence as the correct response. The one who is lazy to think and hasty to speak, however, does not keep quiet even in such situations. Such a person must ultimately, pay dearly for his rashness.

Still, we must note, that the Gemara here praises Rav Ada bar Ahava for his action. He acted for the honor of Hashem, endangering himself in the process. Such zeal is worth many times more than any fines he needed to pay.

[32] **Forgive them** – Likewise, he should tolerate the foolishness of others. Unless spiritual matters are at stake, a person should be quick to overlook mistakes. This does not mean that he allows his family to be reckless. He must certainly train them to treat their belongings with respect. Still, he should be generously tolerant. Thus, he will gain Heaven's goodwill and blessing.

The oil poured out? I will fill your storerooms.

Your clothes were torn? I will satisfy your every request. (BaMidbar Raba 9.2)

CHAPTER FIVE

ETHICS I

Humility

The queen of all ethical behavior is the glorious attribute of humility.

Humility is the best of all attributes. (The Ramban's letter)

A person should first acquire humility,[1] then ask for wisdom and insight – and only then ask for his livelihood.[2] (Tana d'bei Eliyahu Raba 5)

The reward for humility and the awe of Hashem, is wealth, honor and life.[3] (Mishle 22.4)

You heed the desires of the humble, Hashem. (Tehillim 10.17)

Those who are humble inherit the world, and delight in great peace. (Tehillim 37.11)

Raising the Low

When a person humbles himself, when he willingly recognizes that he needs Hashem's salvation in all things, he merits true wealth.

Hashem pronounces his pleasure at the rich man who tithes his income in a concealed way.[4] (Pesachim 113a)

---

[1] **First acquire humility** – True humility is the understanding that all we have, any talent, wisdom and wealth, is only from Hashem. Without such humility, even the person's insight and knowledge are worth little. For how can a person appreciate wisdom, unless he first recognizes the Source of all wisdom?

[2] **Then ask for his livelihood** – Just as wisdom without humility is worth little, so is wealth without wisdom worth very little.

[3] **The reward for humility and the awe of Hashem** – When a person has such attributes, he gains entrance into Hashem's innermost sanctums. He becomes Hashem's trusted companion.

[4] **In a concealed way** – No matter how rich a person is, he still needs Hashem's good favor and blessing. Without this blessing, he neither succeeds nor enjoys his existing wealth. And how may he merit this blessing? – With humility. For when he acts with pride and arrogance, he creates only resentment – the resentment of his fellowmen, as well as the anger of his Maker.

Therefore, he must act humbly. He must conceal his grandeur. When he does mitzvos with his wealth, when he tithes his income, he should do so secretly. Then

"Not because you are great," Moshe told Yisrael, "does Hashem desire you, but because you diminish [and humble] yourselves," (Devarim 7.7)

In contrast...

You diminish those with haughty eyes. (Tehillim 18.28)

R' Avahu taught: It is not the one who is rich today, that will be rich tomorrow, and it is not the one who is poor today, that will be poor tomorrow; rather one Hashem raises, while the other He lowers, as the verse says, "Hashem is Judge, this one He diminishes, this one He elevates." (Tehillim 75.8) (Shmos Raba 31.3)

The verse says: "Let the wise man not pride himself on his wisdom, nor the mighty man on his might, nor the wealthy man on his wealth.[5]

Why? For when such riches do not come from Hashem, they eventually come to an end.[6] (BaMidbar Raba 22.7)

Rav said: The wealth of those who are arrogant, declines and disappears. (Sukka 29b)

Virtue

The land and its contents all belong to Hashem. May a person expect then to prosper when he angers Hashem with his ugly ways?

A good man leaves riches even to his grandchildren,[7] while the sinner's wealth is stored away for the righteous. (Mishle 13.22)

Those He blesses inherit the land, while those He curses, die. (Tehillim 37.22)

The righteous man's activities give him life.[8] (Mishle 10.16)

---

he passes the test of his wealth, gives pleasure to Hashem, and earns himself a full measure of heavenly blessing.

[5] **Nor the wealthy man on his wealth** – If a person's wealth is a gift from Hashem, how can he take pride in it? He received it for nothing. And even if he imagines he earned it himself, how long does he think he may hold onto it? Two thousand years?!

[6] **They eventually come to an end** – The way of the world is that when a person prides himself on that which belongs to another, its real owner comes to reclaim it. Similarly here, Hashem will reclaim His wealth, leaving the proud man with nothing.

[7] **Even to his grandchildren** – Once his wealth is blessed by Hashem, it perpetuates.

Hashem rewards me according to my righteousness; according to the cleanliness of my hands,[9] He compensates me. (Tehillim 18.21)

All the ways of Hashem are kind and true for those who keep His pact. (Tehillim 25.10)

Happy are those who take a whole-hearted approach, those who walk in Hashem's Torah. (Tehillim 119.1)

I was young, also, I have grown old, yet I never saw a righteous man abandoned, or his children begging for bread.[10] (Tehillim 37.25)

The honest man's tent flourishes.[11] (Mishle 14.11)

Hashem gives the virtuous man his desire. (Mishle 10.24)

You [Hashem]
- are kind to the kind;
- to the trusting man, You show Your trust;
- to the pure, You act purely – [however,]
- to the crooked person, You act in crooked ways. (Tehillim 18.26,27)

To the sinner, Hashem gives the task of gathering and amassing wealth, that he may give it to one who is good before Hashem. (Koheles 2.26)

Do not compete with the evil man who wins.[12] (Tehillim 37.7)

That which the wicked man fears, comes upon him.[13] (Mishle 10.24)

---

[8] **Give him life** – That which is righteous is right, in every sense of the word. It is in complete harmony with the world. It matches the person's physical and spiritual constitution, and fills him with glowing health and happiness.

[9] **The cleanliness of my hands** – This is honesty.

[10] **Begging for bread** – The level of a person's heavenly fear affects not only his own, but also his child's livelihood. Conversely, when a person is not righteous, he may well lose this protection, and even bring hunger to his children. *(Ra'vad)*

[11] **The honest man's tent** – While his home is no more than a tent, still he enjoys in it every success and happiness.

[12] **Do not compete with the evil man** – His successes do not follow a natural course, and obviously his mazal is protecting and promoting him. Unless he is threatening others, it is best to leave him alone. Also, no one should feel jealous of him. Eventually his mazal will run its course, and abandon him to his own evils.

[13] **Comes upon him** – The power of the imagination has a special force. When a person focuses on different pictures, vividly, actively, he releases a non-physical force that brings his thoughts to life. Thus, for example, when an ambitious person actively pictures his success, his dreams take on their own reality. They jump out of his mind and into his life.

The wicked man's mansion is destroyed.[14] (Mishle 14.11)

The wicked suffer many injuries, (Tehillim 32.10)

The gains of the wicked lead them to sin.[15] (Mishle 10.16)

Don't trust in force, don't strive in thieving ways, [and] when such wealth flourishes, don't take it to heart.[16] (Tehillim 62.11)

There is a sickly evil I see under the sun, wealth set aside that destroys its owner. That wealth is lost in an evil way. Then when he has a son, he has nothing to give him. (Koheles 5.12,13)

Lust and Greed

One of the greatest obstacles that stands between a person and his dignity, is lust. In the pursuit of self-pleasure, he demeans and humiliates himself completely. His lusts preoccupy and intoxicate him until he has little energy or initiative to accomplish anything productive. A person who wishes to succeed should therefore contain his physical drives. Then he will prosper.

The Torah teaches us proper conduct – that a person should desire to eat meat only when he is wealthy and can well afford it. (Rashi, Devarim 12.20)

Filling one's stomach leads to great sins. (Brochos 32a)

Eight things are detrimental in abundance,[17] but beneficial in moderation; these are traveling, marital relations, *wealth*, work, wine, sleep and hot water.[18] (Gitin 70a)

In the same way, the wicked person brings evil on himself. He lives in a world of wicked people and wicked crimes, and their ugliness is a part of his mind set. The horrors and death scenes that surround him fill his imagination. Then, as these frightful images penetrate his heart, so they are gradually realized.

[14] **The wicked man's mansion** – No matter how solidly he builds it, even when he creates a fortress, it will ultimately break down and disintegrate.

[15] **Lead them to sin** – the greatest tragedy of all!

[16] **Do not take it to heart** – For such wealth does not last for very long.

[17] **Detrimental in abundance** – Wealth in moderation is good. When however, a person has too much wealth, it prevents him from learning Torah. Torah study is the greatest of all mitzvos, and one who doesn't learn when he can, commits a great sin. Of such a person, the Rabbis say, that he loses his share in the world-to-come. Also, abundant wealth leads to haughtiness; another terrible sin. Our Rabbis even equate the haughty man with an idol worshipper. For the arrogant person, instead of serving Hashem, serves only himself. (Rashi. See also 'Pitfalls' p.190)

[18] **Hot water** – for drinking and washing with.

He that loves pleasures shall be a poor man. (Mishle 21.17)

He that indulges in wine and oil, will not be rich. (ibid.)

He who chases after empty people, will have his fill of poverty. (Mishle 28.19)

He who keeps the company of harlots, loses his wealth. (Mishle 29.3)

On account of a prostitute, a man may be drained until he lacks even a loaf of bread. (Mishle 6.26)

Ruddy Wine

Rav Yitzchak said: Wine reddens the face of the wicked in this world, and whitens it[19] in the world-to-come. (Sanhedrin 70a)

Why is the word for wine, 'tirash'?[20] For one who draws after it, becomes 'rash' (poor). (Yoma 76b)

Rav Kahana taught: We see that this word is spelled 'tirash,' while it is pronounced 'tirosh?'[21] This comes to teach that if a person has merits, wine makes him a 'rosh' (a head), whereas if he lacks merits, he becomes 'rash' (poor). (ibid.)

---

[19] **Whitens it** – Consequently, all who indulge excessively in this world's pleasures instead of pursuing mitzvos, suffer great embarrassment.

[20] **Why is wine called 'tirash'?** – Luxury items make a person poorer and not richer. Besides the expenses involved, they tire him; they rob him of his strength and drive, and thereby of prosperity. Thus, to avoid poverty, a person must avoid 'the wine of this world,' the intoxicating self-indulgence that strips him of all.

However, if a person takes from this world in a moderate way, he may enjoy it, and at the same time, enrich himself. This is especially true if he does so with pure intentions. Intentions such as wanting to increase his energy level, or to relax a little and refresh himself, serve to open his mind and help him function with greater efficiency and competence. (Rashi)

[21] **It is pronounced 'tirosh'** – There is nothing fully negative (or positive) in this world. Just as the meaning of the word 'tirash' depends on its pronunciation, so do the effects of wine and the other pleasures of this world, depend on 'their pronunciation' – on why and how a person uses them. When a person uses the elements of this world with proper measures, he will enjoy Heaven's blessings. Moreover, they will even help him get ahead and reach the top.

Taking Care

A person must preserve that which he owns, whether it is his wealth or his health. For if he cannot look after what he already has, what is the point of striving for more?

"...you shall very carefully guard your lives."[22] (Devarim 4.9)

R' Yochanan taught: One whose father left him much money and he wishes to lose it,[23] should:

- wear linen garments,
- use glass vessels and
- leave his workers unsupervised. (Bava Metzia 29b)

R' Chiya said: A person loses three things when he travels[24] – his physical strength, his wealth and his good name. (Breishis Raba 39.11)

Priorities

What should a person do when the preservation of his property costs him his physical well-being? This we should learn from the righteous, who willingly put their wealth before their own comfort and well-being.

When R' Aba Chilkiya would cross a thorny field, he would raise his cloak above his knees so that the thorns would tear his flesh and not his garment.

"Why do you do this?" his students asked.

"My flesh will heal itself," he answered, "but to repair my cloak will cost me time and effort. (Taanis 23b)

"Yakov remained alone ... " He crossed the river again, to bring small jars.

---

[22] **Guard your lives** – This is the first thing a person must guard. He only has one life, and if he loses it, how will he get another one? Also, just as he watches his physical wealth, eating, sleeping and exercising properly, so he must watch his spiritual health. He must surround himself only with that which enriches his total well-being.

[23] **He wishes to lose it** – The Gemara explains that Rebbi Yochanan speaks of the most expensive linens and glass vessels, which are delicate and easily broken. Likewise, leaving workers unsupervised speaks of a situation where they can do much damage.

[24] **When he travels** – A person who is quick to relocate – whether it is changing his job, his home, or even the Torah topic he studies – only loses from his rashness. While there are situations where change is necessary, often he will do better by sticking to what he has started, and seeing it through to the end.

Why did he endanger himself for such items?

From here we learn that the righteous care more for their money, than for themselves.

And why should the righteous love their money so? – Because they don't steal. (Chulin 91a)

Moreover, they treat their children in the same way...

"She wove him a basket of *gomer* (papyrus)."[25] (Shmos 2.3)

Why, the *Gemara* asks, does the Torah mention that she used *gomer*? Surely, this is an irrelevant detail?!

Gomer is a very cheap material, answers the *Gemara*, and this serves to teach that the righteous care more for their money, than for themselves.

And why should the righteous love their money so? – Because they don't steal. (Sota 12a)

Econo-food

The first step a person must take to preserve his physical and material wealth, is not to fall slave to bad habits.

Mar Zutra son of Rav Nachman taught: A person should not accustom his son to meat and wine.[26] (Chulin 84a)

It's enough for a man to live on the milk of his goats and his lambs.[27] (Chulin 84a)

---

[25] **She wove him** – Yocheved, Moshe's mother, made a basket that she may hide him from the Egyptians who were executing all newborn boys. Our Rabbis teach that Yocheved used a cheaper material to save money, although it was of a lesser quality and provided Moshe with less shelter.

Why, we may ask, should this be so? Surely our lives are our most precious assets? We must say that the Torah exaggerates to teach us that a person's property is precious. The work of his hands costs him time. He does not steal it, but rather pays for it with the precious moments of his life. Just as his body is a resource with which he may serve Hashem, so is his property a precious resource that he must use to serve Hashem. He should even risk some of his personal well-being to preserve his wealth.

[26] **Meat and wine** – For once he has a taste for luxurious living, he will depend on it. Then, later in his life, he may even resort to deceit and theft to sustain his sumptuous, opulent lifestyle.

[27] **It's enough** – A person should live economically. Even if he is wealthy, he should be careful with his money. His lambs provide him with wool for clothing; his goats give him milk to drink. If, however, he wants a 'richer' diet, he will have to slaughter his flocks. (Rashi) What then will he live on?

Said Rav Chisda: Neither in my poverty, nor in my wealth, did I eat vegetables.[28] In my poverty I did not eat them, for they arouse the appetite. Now, in my wealth I do not, for I say, "Let meat and fish[29] fill my stomach, instead of vegetables." (Shabbos 140b)

Cleanliness

One important way of earning Heaven's blessings is to appreciate all that Hashem gives us. If we cannot respect and show gratitude for His gifts, how may we expect Him to give us still more?

A person shows just such a respect when he is economical. He also shows it when he keeps clean. By acting in refined ways, he demonstrates how much he appreciates all that Hashem gives him. When however he is slothful, he displays disrespect and ingratitude. This in turn, leads him away from wealth, and brings him to poverty.

Rav Huna taught: One who urinates next to his bed,[30] comes to poverty.

"This refers," Rava said, "to one who does so alongside his bed, but not to one who uses a pot." (Shabbos 62b)

Abaye said: At first I thought that people swept bread crumbs to keep their homes neat; my teacher however told me that the reason is that bread-crumbs under people's feet bring to poverty.

Bread crumbs in the house bring to poverty. On Friday and Tuesday nights unclean forces rest upon them.[31]

---

[28] **Vegetables** – This refers to raw vegetables which arouse his appetite for bread that he cannot afford to buy. (Rashi). However, cooked vegetables are cheap and satisfying. (Tosephos, Eiruvin 55b)

[29] **Meat and fish** – We may explain that Rav Chisda ate sparingly, that he might maximize his Torah study. After all, large quantities of food make a person sleepy, filling his head with fumes that prevent him from learning. He therefore chose meat and fish which are concentrated foods, and high in energy value.

[30] **One who urinates next to his bed** – Why would a person act in so disgustingly? Surely his mind revolts against such behavior? The answer is laziness. It is easier to urinate next to his bed, especially on a cold winter night, than to leave his cozy home. Moreover, he thinks, the sandy floor of his home, will absorb this.

However, indulging one's laziness only leads to loss. It robs a person of anything he gains. If he is lazy to keep his house and other assets in good repair, he soon will have no material wealth. Similarly, if he is lazy to review the Torah he learns, he soon will have no Torah. His laziness will strip him of all!

[31] **On Friday and Tuesday nights** – Traditionally these are nights when most people are at home. And so Hashem, in His goodness, designated these nights as a

The spiritual force appointed over food is called Nakid (Cleanness). The spirit of poverty is called Naval (Filth).[32] (Pesachim 111b)

There was a certain man whom the spirit of poverty[33] pursued. However, this man was very careful with bread-crumbs, and the spirit could not outdo him. Once, the man ate his bread outside, on the grass. "Now," chuckled the spirit, "he has fallen into my hands; surely he won't be able to pick up all those crumbs!"

However, after he finished his meal, the man brought a spade, dug up that grass, and threw it in the river.

He then overheard the spirit wailing, "Woe to me, he has thrown me from his house!" (Chulin 105b)

---

time for rainfall, thereby limiting the inconvenience rain creates. When we have merit, rain falls on these nights, bringing with it great blessings. However, where bread crumbs litter a house, unclean forces rest on them, and prevent these blessings from entering.

[32] **The spirit of poverty** – This is a separate spiritual force.
When Nakid departs from a person's house, his food allowance dwindles. However, one who lacks food, may not yet be poor. He may still live respectably. However, there is a second trouble that comes with slothful behavior. This is that Naval, the spirit of poverty, now enters, bringing with him greater pain and suffering.

[33] **Who the spirit of poverty pursued** – This was the special test that this tzaddik had to face. It may be that in his past he had sinned in this respect, and now he had to cleanse himself. However, once he conquered his inclination to litter, even in difficult situations, the spirit of poverty could no longer test him. The battle was won, and he could now rest.

CHAPTER SIX
ETHICS II

A special area of ethical behavior is showing care and respect to one's fellowman.

Sensitive to Others

Hashem cares for all people as well as He cares for us. Can we then expect His blessings when we constantly step on others' feet?

He who cuts down good trees, sees no success.[1] What is the reason? He upsets other people. (Pesachim 50b)

A holy man passed by a field, and saw its owner clearing it of rocks. The problem was though, he was throwing them in the public way.

"Why do you throw stones from a place that is not yours to a place that is yours?" the holy man rebuked him.

The farmer laughed at these 'silly' words. Still, he did not laugh long – shortly afterwards he lost his field.

One day, as he walked past his old field, he tripped on a rock – one of the rocks he himself had thrown in the road.

"How wise that old man was; I indeed threw stones from property that was not mine, into property that is mine. (Bava Kama 50b)

Theft

A person entering the working world is constantly tempted to use dishonesty as a means of getting ahead. However, he will never succeed through any form of sin. All sin does, is anger Hashem.

Aba Gorion of Tzaidan said in the name of Aba Guria: A person should not teach his son to be a donkey or camel driver, a [traveling] pot-maker, a sailor, a shepherd, or a store-keeper.

Why? For these trades involve theft.[2] (Kidushin 82a)

---

[1] **He who cuts down good trees** – for he angers others. (Rashi)
This is also true when he cuts down his own trees. For when he destroys that which is beneficial and pleasant, others view him as profiting at the public's expense. Such resentment will certainly harm his business endeavors. Spiritually too, their resentment hurts him – and to an even greater degree.

A man does not accumulate wealth from theft.[3] (Medresh Aseres haDibros Dibur 8)

Rav Yosef taught: One who takes merchandise without paying for it, ultimately loses it. (Megilla 6a)

Rav said: The wealth of those who steal, or withhold their workers' wages,[4] declines and disappears. (Sukka 29b)

Wealth made with deceit, diminishes. (Mishle 13.11)

One who oppresses the poor for his own gain, surrenders it to the rich – to his own loss.[5] (Mishle 22.16)

Those who retain paid up documents,[6] lose their wealth. (Sukka 29a)

Do people not decry the thief – even when he steals to fill his hunger?![7] Seven times as much as he stole, he will need to restore. All the wealth of his house he will need to forfeit.[8] (Mishle 6.30,31)

---

[2] **Theft** – In trades where a person must travel from place to place, and pass by other peoples' fields, he is tempted to steal fruit and other produce. Likewise, one who owns a store may be tempted to steal in other ways. If he sells wine, he may be tempted to dilute it with water; if he sells wheat, he may add some dirt to bring up its weight, etc. (Rashi)

[3] **A man does not accumulate wealth from theft** – A thief's objective is to increase his wealth. Using dishonesty, however, only defeats this end.

[4] **Or withhold their workers' wages** – Even if a person only withholds his worker's wages overnight, he sins. (Devarim 24.15)

[5] **To his own loss** – When one person gives to another, there is always some indirect gain he enjoys from this. However, that which he robs from the poor, he gives to the rich, with no gain at all to himself. (Vilna Gaon)

Why, we may ask, should the poor man's money end up in the rich man's lap? We may answer that the terms 'poor' and 'rich' here are not strictly literal. Rather it means that Hashem arranges it that the victim of the crime is one who deserves to suffer a loss, while the one who profits from the incident, deserves a monetary gain. Without the thief sinning, this transfer would still go through. However, since the thief chooses to steal, Hashem uses him for His own heavenly purposes; He ensures that the victim is the 'poor man,' that the recipient is the 'rich man,' while all the thief ends up with, is his sin.

[6] **Paid up documents** – A person is forbidden to keep a credit note or deed once the debtor has paid it. For it may just tempt him to defraud his friend by collecting with it a second time. Therefore, even keeping the note is a dishonest act, and causes him to forfeit Heaven's blessings.

[7] **To fill his hunger** – By stealing from others, he shows an insensitivity to their needs. Likewise, measure for measure, others do not sympathize with the plight that brought him to this crime.

The punishment of the liar is that even when he tells the truth, no one believes him.[9] (Sanhedrin 89b)

Criminal Casualties

One who takes another's money, is as though he spills his blood.[10] (Zohar BaMidbar 219)

Rav Huna says: One who withholds his worker's pay, kills him.[11]

Rav Chisda says: One who withholds his worker's pay, *kills himself*.[12] (Bava Metzia 112a)

Rav Levi taught: The punishment for false measures is more severe than the punishment for illicit relations.[13] (Yevamos 21a)

Why though, we may ask, did people not sympathize with his plight before he stole? Surely, he was already hungry? The answer is that he only came to hunger in the first place, because he had disregarded other peoples' properties. Had he not shown dishonesty even before he was hungry, Hashem would have saved him from this test, and provided him with food in an honest way.

[8] **All the wealth of his house** – It is very hard for a person to erase the negative image he creates in others' minds. He may well have to forfeit all he has, to regain his good name.

[9] **No one believes him** – He loses his trustworthiness, and people do their best to avoid him.

[10] **He spills his blood** – Often a person pours his heart and soul that he may earn his wages. Thus, one who steals his earnings, steals his heart and soul.

[11] **Kills him** – Dishonesty does more than deprive its victim of his wealth. It also disheartens and crushes him, thereby robbing him of his life.

[12] **He kills himself** – Rav Huna and Rav Chisda do not argue. Each one simply emphasizes a different product of dishonesty. Rav Huna speaks of the suffering of the worker. He worked his heart out for his wage. Now after waiting so long, he sees no reward at all. His efforts and energies have all gone to the wind, and this saps him of his life-force. Thus his employer has 'murders' him.

Rav Chisda speaks of the consequences to the thief himself. He enters an underworld of sin, that robs him of life's goodness. This leads to an even worse death – a death of his spirit.

[13] **Illicit relations** – Nearly all forbidden intimacy carries a death penalty. Still, the Rabbis teach, crimes of dishonesty are worse. How can this be?

The Gemara explains that one who has illicit relations may still repent. Thus he cleanses himself of his sin. But when he steals with false measures, it is almost impossible to repent. How and where will he find all the people he cheated?! Thus while the adulterer at the most, suffers death in this world, the thief is saddled with his sin for eternity, a far worse punishment.

Rav Ami taught: The rains only cease because of theft.[14] (Taanis 7b)

The Best Policy

The foundation of honesty is belief in Hashem – belief in His ability to care for us and supply us with all our needs. When a person acts with honesty, he shows how much he trusts in Hashem; and Hashem in turn, blesses his efforts.

An honest man enjoys many blessings.[15] (Mishle 28.20)

Hashem pronounces his pleasure at the poor man who returns a lost item.[16] (Pesachim 113a)

Respecting Others

To succeed in business, a person must act in the best of faith. He must show concern for other peoples' property. For it is better that he loses a little, than that he creates a situation where his friend suffers. Moreover, the person who acts like this, ultimately profits.

One may not save himself, with his friend's property.[17] (Bava Kama 60b)

---

[14] **The rains only cease because of theft** – One who steals actively denies Hashem's ability to provide for all his needs. He turns his back on Hashem, and Hashem in turn, turns His heavenly back on him; He withholds his rains.

[15] **An honest man** – Truth is Hashem's signature. (Shabbos 55a) Thus, the man who acts honestly, adds Hashem's signature to his business ventures. This gives his projects the benefit of Hashem's heavenly endorsement.

[16] **The poor man who returns a lost item** – Hashem desires to bestow on us the best of both worlds. He gladly would make us all millionaires, materially and spiritually. After all, Hashem is certainly not short-handed!! (See BaMidbar 11.23) What then holds Hashem back? – Only that we do not merit yet the full extent of His generosity. We have not acted in ways that bring Hashem pleasure.

The poor man certainly lacks many things, many more than even he realizes. One of these is a fuller trust in Hashem. Returning a lost item to its owner, especially when this owner is a wealthy man, is certainly a test for a poor man.

Hashem tests each person in a different way. The person who is especially prone to fail the test of honesty, is tested with poverty – will he, despite his financial plight, despite his hunger pangs, behave in an ethical way. If he passes this test, he brings himself closer to Hashem and enjoys Hashem's blessings. Thus, when he returns a lost item, or gives charity, or strengthens his faith in some other small way, he gives Hashem great pleasure. This, in turn, removes from him the curse of poverty.

[17] **With his friend's property** – The rule is that one may not damage his friend's property to prevent his own loss, even if he intends refunding this friend for this

R' Yosi said: Care for your friend's money as you would for your own.[18] (Avos 2.12)

The Rabbis said: A person should always be able to mix easily with others.[19] And how may he do this? – By fulfilling every person's wishes.[20] (Kesuvos 17a. Rashi there)

Raban Gamliel b'Rebbi said: If a person is kind to his friend, Heaven is kind to him, but if a person is not kind to his friend, Heaven is not kind to him. (Shabbos 151b)

R' Yehuda said: In the great *beis haknesses* of Alexandria, the gold-smiths sat in one section, the silver-smiths in one section, the black-smiths in one section, the copper-smiths in one section, and the weavers, in one section.

Thus when a poor man entered, he was able to recognize his fellow tradesmen,[21] turn to them, and earn a living from them – for himself and his family. (Sukka 51b)

One who conducts his business dealings in gentle ways, sanctifies Hashem's name. (Yoma 86a)

R' Elazar haKapar taught: One who honors another for his money,[22] ultimately departs from him in shame. (Avos d'R' Noson 29)

---

loss. How much more is this so, if he is not able to compensate his friend for such a loss!

[18] **As you would for your own** – Other people sense when a person genuinely respects them. Moreover, they return this respect, by investing their trust in him. Thus, he who respects others, reaps rich rewards.

[19] **To mix easily with others** – No person can live in isolation. This is especially true of one who lives amongst honest, decent people. If he doesn't follow this rule, troubles will surely follow him.

This rule is important for business situations too. A person should conduct himself with others, even employees, as though he was requesting a favor from them. By giving them this respect, he betters his chances of success.

[20] **Every person's wishes** – A person who respects, honors and loves others, connects with them. However, when he shames or embarrasses them, he creates rifts.

[21] **To recognize his fellow tradesmen** – When a person has others that he can turn to, he is saved. But when he knows no one, who will care for him? Who will save him?

[22] **One who honors another for his money** – The end of this teaching is: One who shames his friend for a mitzva, ultimately, departs from him in honor.

Sensitivities

The Rabbis taught: At first the rich would bring gifts to a mourner's house in baskets of silver and gold, and the poor in baskets of willow. But the poor felt shamed. So the Rabbis enacted, to honor the poor, that all use baskets of willow.[23]

At first they would serve drinks in a mourner's house, to the rich in white *(expensive)* glass, and to the poor in colored *(cheap)* glass. But the poor felt shamed. So the Rabbis enacted, to honor the poor, that all should use colored glass.

At first they would leave the faces of the rich who died uncovered, while the faces of the poor were covered – for they were blackened from starvation. But the poor felt shamed. So the Rabbis enacted, to honor the poor, that all faces should be covered. (Moed Katan 27a)

---

[23] **In honor of the poor** – A person who wishes to truly succeed, must be sensitive even to the poorest members of his society. Thus we find special rules that our leaders made through the generation. These serve to teach us how we too, should worry about the feelings of those less fortunate than ourselves.

CHAPTER SEVEN
GREAT PEOPLE I

Not Cheap

The attribute of greatness goes together with wealth. It teaches a person to think in large terms. This has many positive results; one is that he doesn't cheapen himself in his drive for material success.

R' Eliezer said: When a man owns a million, and they take all his money from him, he shouldn't cheapen himself over a small coin.[1] (Avos d'R' Noson 15)

Those who take the best share, see no success.

What is the reason? They upset other people.[2] (Pesachim 50b)

There were two very wealthy men in the world, one from Yisrael and one from the world's nations. They were Korach, a *Yisrael*; and Haman, a gentile. Both were destroyed. Why? – For their wealth did not come as a gift from Hashem; rather they snatched it.[3] (BaMidbar Raba 22.7)

---

[1] **He shouldn't cheapen himself** – Hashem gives a person dignity, and he must do his best to preserve it. Thus he may not act in greedy or other demeaning ways.
A person who snatches, lowers himself in others' eyes. Moreover, he awakens their resentment and hatred, and alienates himself from them. And since no person can live alone, since no person can exist in a vacuum, the greedy person heads only for failure.

[2] **They upset other people** – Those who always take the best share, fluster the world's sense of justice. For it is unfair that one person should always receive a superior portion. The arrogance of one who demands this, only creates resentment.
An extension of this idea is, that a person should not focus only on increasing his own wealth. He should also concern himself with the welfare and wealth of those around him. As he grows greater, he should take care that others benefit from his new riches.

[3] **They snatched it** – Snatching and greediness does more than degrade a person and spoil his chances for success. As we see with both Korach and Haman, it ultimately, even destroys him.

Don't Grab

One who seeks a prosperous life, must train himself not to grab. For when he grabs from others, he thinks of them as his source of wealth. Thus, he moves away from believing in Hashem. Ultimately, he will prosper better if he owns less now, and waits for Hashem's blessings to enrich him, later.

He who hates gifts[4] will live. (Mishle 15.27)

Moshe said: Not one donkey did I take from them.[5] (BaMidbar 16.15)

[Likewise] Shmuel said to the people of *Yisrael*: Answer me before Hashem ... whose ox have I taken, or whose donkey have I taken? ... from whose hand have I accepted a bribe? (Shmuel 1.12.1,3)

Buy your own food and drink, Hashem told the Jewish people as they traveled the deserts, don't behave like paupers[6] but rather like the rich ...

---

[4] **He who hates gifts** – Conversely, one who loves gifts, who lives only for handouts, will die.

One who aspires to wealth should abhor taking from others. This doesn't mean that he cannot accept gifts. If he needs help, and doesn't take it, he is an arrogant fool. Still, he shouldn't contrive to receive or enjoy taking gifts; he should hate the thought of depending on others.

[5] **Not one donkey** – We see that the greatest leaders of Yisrael avoided taking from others. Instead, every act they did was an act of giving. This explains how they gained such greater powers, such an influence – an influence we feel right to today!

[6] **Don't behave like paupers** – While Yisrael had spent many years in Egypt living as slaves, they left with a great wealth – they had gold, silver, fine jewelry and garments, as well as large herds. Moreover, Hashem would daily send them their needs, mann from the Heavens, the miraculous well of water, as well as flying fowl. Why then should Hashem command them to buy their own food and drink? Surely with their great wealth, they would have little inclination to invade and plunder the surrounding nations?

Yisrael left Egypt as a victorious army. As such, it was easy to act as most conquering armies act – namely, to terrorize and despoil the districts they marched through. If you can get if for free, why should you pay? Hashem, however, wanted them to act in a moral, exalted way. Therefore He forbade such conduct.

Similarly, not all people who are rich, think and behave in large ways. They are not all generous and gracious. If they can get something for free, they happily take it. This, however, is not a 'large' way of acting, and does not lead to greatness. Instead, it keeps them away from any lasting success.

that you do not shame or deny the blessings Hashem sends you.[7] (Devarim 2.7, Rashi there)

One who has two meals should not take from the community kitchen.[8] (Peah 8.7)

R' Akiva said, "Make your Shabbos like a weekday,[9] and don't depend on your fellowman." (Shabbos 118a)

Rav Noson bar Abba said: All who hope to the tables of others, live in a darkened world.[10]

---

[7] **That you do not shame or deny** – One who has today's needs, is already wealthy in a certain sense. Such a person should strive not to take from others. Even he is only wealthy for today, i.e., he has today's needs, he should not take for tomorrow. Who then will feed him tomorrow? The One who provides him with his needs today. Moreover, when a person trusts Hashem to supply him with his daily needs, besides acquiring greatness for himself, he merits special heavenly blessings. He is able to tap into the 'Source of all Wealth.'

On the other hand however, a person who 'sponges' or 'snatches' from others, shows himself to be in need and poor. This in turn shames Hashem; it indicates that Hashem cannot provide these people – the people who keep His Torah and mitzvos – with their needs.

[8] **One who has two meals** – A rich man is a giver, a poor man a taker. This principle is ingrained into every person's thought. Even when a poor man gives, others automatically see him as 'rich'. On the other hand, when a rich man takes, they look at him with some amusement. "Maybe he isn't so rich after all," they think.

[9] **Make your Shabbos like a weekday** – One who keeps Shabbos shows that he trusts Hashem to feed and sustain him. Thus it is no problem for him to stop working. Beyond this, when he honors Shabbos, when he glorifies it with choice dishes and delicacies, with expressions of joy and delight for Hashem's many kindnesses, he trumpets Shabbos's triumph: "Look world, Hashem is my shepherd!!" This itself leads to a great wealth. (See also 'Shabbos' p.134)

However, if he must take from others to honor Shabbos, in a sense, he defeats the purpose. That he must rely on others, indicates that Hashem is not taking care of his needs!! Therefore he is better off by making do with a minimum. This sacrifice itself gives honor to the holy Shabbos.

Also, he may still honor Shabbos, in a small way. If he adds just one extra treat – something he does not allow himself during the week – this too adds to Shabbos's glory. For more important than the delicacies a person buys for Shabbos, is the joy and delight he gives this holy day.

[10] **In a darkened world** – Every man needs a source of sustenance, a place from where he draws his daily bread. Once a person identifies this source, his eyes turn

Rav Chisda said: Their lives are no life.[11] (Beitza 32b)

The community pays no attention[12] to one who commands, Do not bury me from my own estate.[13] We do not allow him to enrich his children, by having the community pay his burial expenses. (Kesuvos 48a)

One who need not take, and takes, does not leave the world without depending on others; but one who may take, yet doesn't, does not die of old age, without feeding others.[14] (Peah 8.8)

Ribis

There is a certain type of taking that the Torah forbids completely. This is ribis,[15] charging interest for the money one Yisrael lends another. While a

---

to it. He looks here for his daily bread, and the other 101 things he needs. He hopes and waits for it.

The true source of all sustenance is only Hashem. However, this is not obvious to all. Hashem disguises Himself. He makes it appear that our sustenance comes from elsewhere. The person's challenge is to see through this facade, and realize that he must hope only to Hashem.

One who meets this challenge – who sees through the mask – lives in Hashem's light. He trusts in Hashem, and Hashem meets his trust by providing him with his every need. On the other hand, one who 'hopes to the table of others,' who looks to his fellowman for his business and worldly successes, does not see Hashem – he does not appreciate Hashem's light.

[11] **Their lives are no life** – The tragedy of such people is a great one. For as long as they bind themselves to rich relatives and other charities, as long as they await their generosity and mercy, they do not really live. As long as they bind themselves to 'false saviors,' they are blind to Hashem. They remain in a prison – slaves to those who feed him.

[12] **The community pays no attention** – The attribute of greed borders even on madness. Thus, just as no one listens to the madman, no one listens to the man who is greedy for unjust gain.

[13] **Do not bury me from my own estate** – A person must learn to pay his own way, and not sponge on others. He must use his own resources to buy what he needs, and try not to profit from others. Such an income violates the rules of human dignity, and ultimately, must fail. It must make him only the poorer.

[14] **Without feeding others** – One who appreciates that he need not take from others, easily understands that what he gives to others, does not impoverish him. He waits only for Hashem to feed him, and is generous with the little he has. Hashem, in turn, rewards such an attitude richly. Since he does not take, Hashem makes him a giver.

[15] Ribis – Practically this term means, increment, the profit a person gains when he lends his wealth. Another term for such interest is neshech, which means "bite."

person may rent his car, his house, or even his coat, he may not rent out his money. The Torah wishes us to act kindly with each other, and if "all is business," what room is left for kindness? This is one reason why the Torah forbids us to earn such a fee from fellow-Yisrael.

R' Yitzchak taught: Better off is one who owns only ten zehuvim (gold coins),[16] doing business and sustaining himself with them, than one who borrows larger sums with ribis. As people say, one who borrows with ribis, loses both what is his, and what is not his. (VaYikra Raba 3.1)

Still, our Rabbis teach, the lender suffers even more than the borrower.

When a person in his lust for wealth, lends money with ribis, a curse is placed on his property.[17] (Tanchuma, BeHar 1)

Those who lend money with interest, their wealth is confiscated. (Sukka 29a)

He who increases his wealth with ribis, gathers it for the man who is kind to the poor.[18] (Mishle 28.8)

Rava said: Those who lend with interest are like murderers[19] – just as a murderer cannot restore what he takes, so one who lends with ribis cannot restore what he takes. (Bava Metzia 61b)

One who lives on ribis in this world, does not live in the world-to-come. (Shmos Raba 31.6)

R' Avahu taught: In this world, the wicked who eat the proceeds of ribis, are wealthy and live serenely,[20] while the righteous are poor.

This name points to the idea that ribis is like a snake bite. While it makes only a small wound, gradually it affects a person's whole body, until eventually, it kills him. (Rashi, Shmos 22,24)

[16] Zehuvim – This is possibly the modern day equivalent of a few thousand dollars; hardly a large amount with which to start a business. Still, a person will do better with a small amount that meets with the Hashem's approval, than large sums that contravene Torah law.

[17] **A curse is placed on his property** – The misuse of wealth draws a curse down on it, first weakening and finally destroying it.

[18] **The man who is kind to the poor** – When money does not come from Heaven's blessing, but is the product of greedy snatching, its owner derives no benefit. For Hashem transfers the wealth from the person who misuses it, to the person who uses it correctly.

[19] **Like murderers** – Also, just as kindness lengthens peoples lives, so a lack of kindness, shortens them. This then is another reason why one, who instead of lending money for free, lends it with interest, is like a murderer.

But in the future, when Hashem will open the vaults of Gan Aden, the wicked will bite their teeth into their own flesh ... and cry, "If only we had been common laborers carrying loads on our shoulders, if only we had been slaves ... that we may merit to share in such rewards. (Shmos Raba 31.5)

Conversely, keeping the laws of ribis leads to great blessings...

R' Avahu taught: One who is wealthy, gives charity to the poor and does not lend money with *ribis,* is counted as though he fulfilled *all the Torah's mitzvos.* (Shmos Raba 31.4)

R' Avahu taught that when Shlomo built the *Beis haMikdash,* he prayed to Hashem:[21] "Master of the Universe, when a person asks You for wealth, and You know that it will harm him (for he will transgress the laws of *ribis*), do not listen to his prayer; however if You see him using his riches in pleasant, kind ways, give him *all that he asks for!* (Shmos Raba 31.5)

Give and Take

In general, one who gives, gains power and control; while one who takes, loses them. An act of giving strengthens a person. An act of taking weakens him.

A rich man rules over the poor. (Mishle 22.7)

A borrower is a slave to the man who lends to him. (ibid.)

Shame

At times it seems that the giver humiliates himself, while the taker rises higher and higher. In truth though, the taker's self-indulgence mocks and lowers him before the giver.

The Rabbis taught that the mitzva of tzedaka is to give the poor man all that he lacks ... even a horse to ride on and a slave to run before him.

---

[20] **In this world, the wicked are wealthy** – Worse than Hashem stripping a sinner of his wealth, is when Hashem allows him to keep it. For He then encourages him to continue in his evil ways, and causes him to lose his world-to-come.

[21] **He prayed to Hashem** – Thus, one who observes the laws of ribis carefully, has the prayer of Shlomo haMelech promoting his success – even in this world!

Of Hillel, they say, that he would provide a poor man who had once been wealthy, a horse to ride on[22] and a slave to run before the horse. Once they had no runner, so Hillel himself ran in front of the horse, for twelve miles! (Kesuvos 67b)

Great Expenses

Like attracts like. Poverty attracts poverty; and wealth attracts wealth. Thus the wealthy who act in wealthy ways, come to greater wealth; while the poor who are miserly, simply become poorer.

Rava asked Raba bar Mari: "What is the source for the folk-saying, 'poverty follows the poor'?"

"We learn," he answered, "that the wealthy brought their first fruits in gold and silver baskets, [the *Kohanim* thereafter returned their baskets to them]. The poor however, brought their first fruits in willow baskets, and gave the fruit *with the basket*." (Bava Kama 92a)

Rava asked Raba bar Mari: "From where do we learn that one who touches oil, has oily hands?" [i.e., one who mixes with the wealthy, becomes rich][23]

---

[22] **A horse to ride on** – True tzedaka entails giving a person all his needs, even his psychological ones. This pauper needed a horse and a runner. He could not live without them. So Hillel provided him even with this.

Obviously, Hillel as Yisrael's leading sage had a duty to preserve his own dignity. However, since he could find no other to do this mitzva, and since this mitzva is Hashem's command, he saw no option but to do it himself.

Can there be anything lower than running before a horse and rider? Surely, Hillel dropped to a new low? – History however, tells us that Hillel remained a prince to his people, while this pampered pauper, who was so hooked on his own importance, lost all dignity. By allowing Hillel to run before him, he became a source of ridicule for all time.

[23] **One who mixes with the wealthy, becomes rich** – When one spends time amongst the rich, he learns to adopt their attitudes and attributes, their mode of behavior, speech and even, thought. All this helps him to gain his own wealth.

In a metaphysical sense too, the person who associates with the rich, "rubs shoulders" with the heavenly or sometimes, 'unheavenly' forces that enrich them. Obviously, wealth that comes with Heaven's blessing is better than that which comes with a curse. Therefore, if he wishes to gain riches in this way, he should associate only with people whose wealth is kosher, while he avoids people whose wealth comes through sin.

"We learn this from Lot," he answered, "as the verse states, 'Lot who followed Avram had flocks, herds and tents.' (Breishis 13.5)" (Bava Kama 93a)

Rav Acha ben Yakov said: There is no poverty in a place of wealth.[24] (Shabbos 102b)

---

[24] **A place of wealth** – The place of wealth here refers specifically to the Mishkan, the mobile Temple that Yisrael built in the desert. Here Hashem rested His Divine Presence, thereby designating it as a place of His glory and wealth. Accordingly, its construction was large and opulent.

In the same spirit, a person who aspires to success, should not act in a poor way. Rather, he must learn to be generous, to display charity and largesse. While squandering is ugly, and he must treat his property with respect, still he cannot be mean. We may praise economy, but not when it is at the expense of friendliness, kindness, cleanliness, etc., and especially, not at the expense of mitzvos.

The question then is when must a person be sparing, and when must he be generous? – One idea is that spending that comes from positive attributes, that comes from a love for Hashem's mitzvos or his fellowman, leads to further blessings. However, spending that comes from laziness or lust, brings to poverty. A person should avoid such expenditures at all cost.

Thus, if a person wants a new suit to honor the festivals, this is a good motive, and will enrich him; but if he wants the suit to indulge his ego, he would do better to save his money. Likewise, if he buys rich foods, to honor his guests, his investment pays him rich dividends; but if they serve only to feed his appetites, he is only the poorer for his weakness.

CHAPTER EIGHT
GIVING

My People

There is a built-in connection between Heaven's blessings and the attribute of giving; the one depends on the other. The reason for this is that Hashem gives a person wealth not only to take care of himself, but also for the benefit of others.

The verse says "Lend My people money."

"And who are Your people?" *Yisrael* asks Hashem.

"The poor," He answers.[1] (Shmos Raba 31.5)

"Riches and honor, that's all Mine," [says Hashem,] "rare treasuries and *open-handedness*."[2] (Mishle 8.18)

The way of a man is that if someone has wealth, he hides himself from his poor relatives. He even disowns them. Hashem however, does not act so, He protectively hovers over them. (Shmos Raba 31.5)

Follow Me

More than Hashem wants the poor to receive, He wants us to give to them.

R' Yitzchak said: "Those who run to do *tzedaka*,[3] Hashem readies money for them that they may do *tzedaka*.

Throw your bread on the waters – you will find eventually that it returns to you.[4] (Koheles 11.1,2)

---

[1] **The poor** – Since Hashem is closest to those who are in pain, He therefore has a very special relationship with the poor.

[2] **Rare treasuries and open-handedness** – Hashem, as Creator and Owner of the world, is certainly wealthy. We see though, that He only values His wealth when it stands next to His great generosity. This is His pride, and He equates it to His other great qualities – His power and His might. Giving, in Hashem's eyes, is an essential element of Divine nobility.

[3] **Those who run to do tzedaka** – Hashem directs his tzedaka funds to those who pursue tzedaka. This is logical. Hashem wishes people to do charity, and he therefore provides them with the means to do this. The person who is quickest to fulfill this duty, is the person Hashem is quickest to enrich.

R' Avahu said: "The gift of man enriches him" (Mishle 18) – that which he gives the poor,[5] helps him succeed. (Shmos Raba 31.2)

"Is the pauper not the one who 'thinks poor', i.e., he is miserly; and is not the wealthy man the one who 'thinks rich,' i.e., he is generous?"[6] (Kesuvos 68a)

Wealth does not help against Hashem's wrath, however charity saves a person from death.[7] (Mishle 11.4)

Generosity

Hashem not only gives us resources to benefit others, He also seeks our benefit – He wants us to learn the attribute of generosity. This, however, is a tough lesson. A person has a natural selfishness that holds him back from giving.

There is a special advantage a selfish person enjoys. For he makes a great sacrifice when he gives; and the greater this sacrifice, the greater is its worth. Still, to receive a full heavenly blessing, he must change his self; he must become a giving person.

---

[4] **It returns to you** – What of the person who gives away more than the share Heaven expects him to give? We learn here that even when he gives away his own food, and even when this is to those that have no merit, Heaven ensures that all eventually returns to him. Still, a person may not be reckless. As he is careful to invest his money intelligently, so he has a duty to seek out worthy causes, and give them his major support.

[5] **That which he gives the poor** – The poorer the person, the greater is the pleasure the gift gives him; and the greater his pleasure, the greater is Heaven's pleasure. Thus, the giving person has to look especially for those who are most in need.

[6] **One who 'thinks rich'** – A person's attitude to the poor determines how rich or poor he really is. For it is not only a person's material possessions that define his wealth. A man may have much money, and still be a miserable pauper. If he is miserly, he lacks the appreciation of what money is and what it can do. Thus he does not enjoy his money. He is like the man who owns an expensive piece of technology, but has no idea how to use it – he may as well not possess it at all. Similarly, when a person has money and doesn't help others with it, it is as though he doesn't have it. Thus he is really a pauper.

On the other hand, one who is wisely generous, enjoys his resources to the full. While he may not own much, still he is wealthy. He possesses one of the richest of all attributes – the ability to give. Moreover, measure for measure, Hashem refills his pockets, richly!

[7] **Charity saves a person from death** – Bank accounts, stocks and shares do little to help a person in his grave. Only the charity he gives, buys him eternity.

People curse the one who holds back his grain,[8] while they pour blessings on the head of he who sells freely. (Mishle 11.26)

There is one who scatters his wealth, yet gains more; while the one who is mean, becomes destitute. (Mishle 11.24)

If you see a man scattering his money to charity, know that he is becoming richer. (Shocher Tov, Mishle 11)

He that has a generous eye shall be blessed, for he gives *his bread* to the poor.[9] (Mishle 22.9)

When Hashem loves a person, He sends him a gift. What is this? A pauper to *give* him merit.[10] (Zohar, Breishis 104)

Raban Gamliel b'Rebbi taught: He who is kind to others, Heaven is kind to him;[11] but he who is not kind to others, Heaven is not kind to him. (Shabbos 151b)

He who is gracious to the poor, lends to Hashem;[12] Hashem will surely pay him back. (Mishle 19.17)

Spilling Over

When a person is generous, his children learn to be generous too. Thus, they too eat the fruit of his righteousness.

R' Yehoshua ben Levi said: "All who accustom themselves to do tzedaka, merit sons who are wise, wealthy and loved..." (Bava Basra 9b)

---

[8] **The one who holds back his grain** – He withholds his stocks from the market until market prices rise. Little does he know that his selfish intents hurt himself more than they hurt others. He loses the favor of his fellowman, and thereby, of Hashem. All he receives is a round of curses.

[9] **He gives his bread to the poor** – The gift that comes off the person's own plate, is the most worthy gift of all.

[10] **A pauper to give him merit** – A person must learn to appreciate the chance to help others; he must train himself to view it as a gift. When such an opportunity comes his way, our Rabbis teach, it should make him very happy – as though he had received a great prize.

[11] **Heaven is kind to him** – The rewards for charity follow a simple equation.

[12] **He lends to Hashem** – Moreover, another verse tells us, "The borrower enslaves himself to the lender" (Mishle 22.7). From these two verses the Gemara learns that Hashem so to speak, enslaves Himself to the one who helps the poor. (Bava Basra 10a)

Growth

The charity a person gives, has a direct influence on his income – like fertilizer on a plant.

> Rav Avira taught: "If a person sees that his income is shrinking,[13] let him convert it to charity – how much the more then, should he give it, when his income grows. (Gitin 7b)

> Mar Zutra said: A pauper, although he himself receives charity, should give charity; through this he rids himself of his poverty.
> On this Rav Yosef commented: The marks of his poverty disappear.[14] (Gitin 7b)

A Promise of Wealth

Every person has an obligation to tithe his wealth, to dedicate a tenth of his capital, as well as his subsequent gains, to holy causes – especially to Torah study.[15]

At first glance it would appear that tithing one's income is a mitzva that depletes a person's wealth. Our Rabbis however, teach us that on the contrary, not only does it protect his property, it even enhances and increases it.[16]

---

[13] **If a person sees that his income is shrinking** – A person who sees his income shrinking, should realize that this may be through a lack of charity. The remedy then must be to give more. Thus, he may halt its fall, and even reverse this downward trend.

[14] **The marks of his poverty disappear** – Even when a person gives a small amount of charity, this already helps him. In the merit of his tzedaka, he receives wealth. (Maharsha)

[15] **Every person has an obligation** – Our Rabbis teach that a mitzva a person fulfills out of duty is worth more than a mitzva he does voluntarily, (Kidushin 31a). Thus, when he tithes his income because this is a Torah requirement, this carries more merit than the charity he does from a sense of nobility. As such, it has a greater power to enrich him.

[16] **It even enhances and increases it** – When a person gives a cut of his profits to heavenly causes, he effectively makes Hashem a partner in his enterprise. This automatically enhances his business. Moreover, since his business is now furthering Hashem's interests, the whole business takes on the character of a mitzva and gives him a special merit. (Ahavas Chesed 2.20)

R' Akiva said: Tithing is a fence for wealth.[17] (Avos 3.13)

"Rebbi," asked R' Yishmael b'Rebbi Yosi, "How do the wealthy of *Eretz Yisrael* merit their wealth?"

"Through tithing their income," he answered. (Shabbos 119a)

Rav Nachman bar Yitzchak said: If a person gives his tithes, he becomes wealthy. (Brochos 63a)

Who merits that his prayers go up to the Heavens and bring down the rains? – He who gives his tithes. But he who does not give his tithes, does not merit prayers that go up to Heaven and bring down the rains; instead they remain bound in the clouds.[18] (BaMidbar Raba 12.11)

Try It

Rav Yochanan came upon the nephew of Reish Lakish. "What verse are you learning?" he asked him.

"A'ser t'aser,[19] (you shall give a tenth of your produce)" the youth replied.

"How do we interpret 'a'ser t'a'ser'?" the boy then asked, "Why is the word doubled?"

"A'ser, give a tenth, and t'a'sher, you will become rich," R' Yochanan answered.

"How do you know this works?" asked the boy.

"Try it," said R' Yochanan.

"Surely we are forbidden to test Hashem?!"

"This is an exception," the R' Yochanan answered, "as the verse says "Bring all the tithes to the storeroom, that there may be food in My home, and please test me on this," says Hashem, "if I don't open for you the windows of Heaven, and empty my blessings to you 'ad bli dai.'[20]" (Malachi 3.10)

---

[17] **A fence for wealth** – It protects his property from being invaded by thieves and other types of mishap.

[18] **They remain bound up in the clouds** – Hashem will not condone the behavior of one who does not give his tithes. Therefore, He ignores his prayers, and withholds His heavenly blessings.

[19] A'ser – The word a'ser literally means take a tenth.

[20] 'Ad bli dai' – Literally these words translate as ad (until), bli (without), dai (enough). While the way to understand this is 'without measure.' Still the unusual phrasing indicates that we extend the interpretation. Thus, we interpret the word

"And what does *'ad bli dai'* mean?" Rami bar Chama asked

"*Ad she'yib'lu sifso'sei'chem mi'lomar dai,*" – until your lips wear away from crying: Enough! Enough! (Taanis 9a)

'A'ser t'a'ser' – Give tithes that you may be rich! Give tithes that you do not lose your wealth![21] (Parshas Reah, Tanchuma)

Rich and Poor

Hashem wants givers. Give, and Hashem will supply you with all your needs. Cease from giving, and Hashem will give your livelihood to another, so that he may sustain you and thereby, fulfill Hashem's will.

R' Yehuda haNasi taught: When the pauper asks the rich man for food, if he feeds him, all is well. But if not, the verse teaches: "The rich and the poor meet,[22] Hashem makes them all." (Mishle 22) – He who makes this one rich, may make him poor; He who makes this one poor, may make him rich. (Temura 16a)

If you merit money, use it for *tzedaka*; thus, you buy yourself this world, and inherit the world-to-come; but if you do not use it for *tzedaka*, you may suddenly find that it has flown away. (Derech Eretz Zuta 4)

'bli' as 'balu,' (your lips are worn out). The verse now reads 'until your lips wear away from saying "Enough!"'

This teaching is a triumph for the Torah way. Here we are told that we may actually test Hashem to see if he enriches us. All we need do is carefully tithe our produce (and other income), and we will enjoy wealth – a wealth we can see with our eyes, a wealth that even leads us to cry out, "Enough! Enough!"

[21] **That you will not lose** – If tithes enrich a person, surely then they protect him from losing his wealth? The answer is that sometimes, for a number of other reasons, a person must lose his wealth. Giving tithes however, protects him from such loss. (Ahavas Chesed 2.19)

[22] **The rich and the poor meet** – This rule that the rich have a duty to the poor, applies wherever there are rich and poor. Thus Rebbi Noson applies this principle to Torah study:

If the student goes to his rebbi and the rebbi teaches him, Hashem enlightens the eyes of both of them; if not, "...the rich and the poor meet, Hashem enlightens them both." (Mishle 29.13) He who made this one wise, may make him foolish. He who made this one foolish may make him wise. (Temura 16a)

A teacher too has much to learn. When he teaches others, he also merits to learn new things. If however, the teacher selfishly puts his own studies first, he only ends up poorer. (Rashi)

R' Avahu taught: Hashem tests the rich man – Will he open his hand to the poor? If he passes his test, he may enjoy his wealth in this world, while the reward for his *mitzvos* awaits him in the world-to-come. But if he is mean, he and his money are destroyed, even in this world. (Shmos Raba 31.2)

If you do not give to your poor brother, ultimately you will have to receive from him. But if you give him once, you will merit to give him – even hundred times.[23] (Sifri Re'ah 116)

Beware

On the other hand, the punishment for those who refuse to fulfill their duty, may be quite horrible.

One who blocks his ears from the poor man's cry – he too [ultimately] will call out, and no one will answer. (Mishle 21.13)

R' Avahu said: Why is Babylon called Shinar? For it shakes out its wealthy.

On this the *Gemara* comments: And even though we see wealthy men there, their wealth does not last for three generations.[24] (Zevachim 113b)

Chizkiya ben Parnach said in the name of R' Yochanan: Why is the section on tithes placed next to the section that deals with the unfaithful wife? – To teach that one who avoids giving the *Kohen* his tithes,[25]

---

[23] **Even hundred times** – Is there another investment that offers such good returns?

[24] **Their wealth does not last** – They lose their wealth, for they show no mercy to their fellow-man. This accords with the teaching (Beitza 32b): The wealthy men of Babylon are heading for Gehinom. (Rashi)

While they may enjoy their wealth for these three generations, this is nothing to a soul that must suffer for its sins eternally!

[25] **The Kohen his tithes** – In the times of the Temple, a householder gave two types of gifts. One was to the Kohanim [and Leviim]; the other, to the poor. The gifts of the Kohanim however, were not charity in the normal sense. Rather, they supported them, so that they could devote their lives to serving Hashem. This system, in turn, benefitted the householder. It bought him a share in Hashem's holy service.

Thus, the Kohen depended on the householder. He needed his tithes to feed his family. This dependency was a kindness Hashem had done the community of Yisrael. He had arranged the economy such that every member of Yisrael could have a stake in their heavenly mission.

Still, should the householder refrain from this duty, should he hold back his dues, Hashem would involve him in the community's cause in a different way – He ultimately depends on the *Kohen* because of his wife.[26] Moreover, he himself becomes poor, and depends on the tithes of others. (Brochos 63a)

Hashem gives wealth to people that they may feed the poor and do *mitzvos*; if they do not use it in this way, and [moreover] they act haughtily, they are whipped.[27] (Zohar, Breishis 121)

R' Yochanan ben Zakkai and his students once saw a young woman gathering barley grains from amongst animal droppings. When she saw him, she wrapped herself with her hair,[28] and approached him.

"Rebbi, please feed me," she said.

"Who are you, my daughter?" he asked.

"Nakdimon ben Gorion's daughter," she answered.

"What happened to your family's money?" he asked.

"Rebbi," she replied, "do they not say in Yerushalayim, that the salt of money[29] is giving it away."

"And your father-in-law's money?" he asked.

"The one wealth destroyed the other.[30]

"Rebbi," she continued, "Do you remember signing my wedding contract?"

---

would make the householder depend on the Kohen. Moreover, as a further punishment, Hashem would impoverish the householder such that he himself now depended on the second type of tithe – the gifts of the poor.

[26] **Because of his wife** – One who suspects his wife of having adulterous relations, must bring her up to the Temple that the Kohen may test her. This also involves bring a sacrifice, a gift to the Kohen.

And why, we may ask, should she suffer? The reason is that it is she encourages him to withhold his tithes. (Imrei Yakar)

[27] **They are whipped** – There is even a physical danger in not fulfilling one's spiritual duties.

[28] **She wrapped herself with her hair** – She was so poor that she needed to wrap herself with her hair to present herself before Rebbi Yochanan.

[29] **The salt of money** – Salt is a preservative. It saves food from spoiling. In the same way, spending money on charity saves it from being lost. Thus, a person who wishes to preserve his property, must use it to help others. (Rashi). While Nakdimon was a very religious man, he did not give sufficient charity. Now his daughter needed to search for her food amongst animal droppings.

[30] **The one wealth destroyed the other** – The acts one person does, influences and changes the behavior of others. Nakdimon did not fulfill his duties to the community, and the rest of the family followed him in his neglect. Therefore they also lost their wealth.

"I remember," R' Yochanan told his students, "that I read there of a dowry of a million golden *zuz*, excluding the gifts from her father-in-laws' house.

"Fortunate are you, Yisrael,"[31] cried R' Yochanan, "when you do Hashem's will, no nation can touch you; but when you don't do Hashem's will, you are at the mercy of lowly people; and not only at their mercy, but at the mercy of their animals.[32]

The Gemara asks: Did Nakdimon ben Gorion not do charity? Surely when he would go to the *Beis haMedresh* they would spread fine carpets before him, and afterwards the poor would fold them up and take them. Is this not charity?

"We may say," answers the Gemara, "that he did this only for his honor;[33] or we may say that while he gave charity, this was not in line with his wealth – as people say: The larger the camel,[34] the greater its load." (Kesuvos 66b)

Carefully, Tactfully

The obligation to give charity is an obligation to make peace in the world. For the pain of the poor is a very great pain.

---

[31] **Fortunate are you, Yisrael** – Still we may ask, is this punishment not too severe? We may answer that had Hashem not loved Nakdimon, Nakdimon may well have escaped this drastic turn of fortune. However, since Hashem loved Nakdimon, Hashem would not allow him and his family to live with their mistake. He therefore punished them for their neglect in this world, thus helping them to atone for their wrongs. This, ultimately, is a greater kindness than allowing Nakdimon to keep his wealth. It also explains why Rebbi Yochanan declared that Yisrael is fortunate even when they don't do Hashem's will!

[32] **But at the mercy of their animals** – Only those grains that the animals in their indolence had not digested properly, could she salvage for herself.

[33] **He did this only for his honor** – While giving charity with a motive such as healing the ill, or eternal reward, counts as a full mitzva (Bava Basra 10b), giving charity for honor has little merit. This is because the act of kindness is an act of faith, an act of glorifying Hashem. With it a person declares his belief in Hashem; he asserts that all he need do is fulfill Hashem's desires. However, when he gives charity for self-glory, he undoes this goal and robs the charity of its spiritual worth.

[34] **The larger the camel** – A camel driver loads his camel to the maximum before he embarks on a long, expensive desert journey. Similarly, when Hashem sends a person into this world, He wants him to perform to full capacity. While Nakdimon gave large sums to charity, he may not have toiled over this according to his financial strengths.

R' Yitzchak said, "One who gives a *p'rutah* to a poor man, receives six blessings; one who appeases him with words, receives a further eleven blessings.[35] (Bava Basra 9b)

R' Yehuda b'Rebbi Simon said: The poor man sits and raves: "How am I less than So-and-so? Yet he sleeps on his bed, while I sleep here! He sleeps in his house, while I am here!

"If you arise and supply him his needs, says Hashem, "...I will count this as though you have made peace between Me and him."[36] (VaYikra Raba 34.16)

Woe to the person about whom the pauper complains to his Master – for the poor man is closer to the King than all of them.[37] (Zohar, Shmos 86)

One who shouts at a poor person, shouts at the Divine Presence. (Zohar, Shmos 86)

Atonements

Sometimes, despite the kindness and charity a person does, he still suffers poverty. One reason for this may be that he needs the atonement of poverty to cleanse himself of sin. The wealth he must lose, works to redeem him of his heavenly debts.

R' Yishmael said: Come and see how much compassion the Creator has for a person – He allows the person who sins, to redeem himself with money.[38] (Mechilta Mishpatim 21.109)

---

[35] **Eleven blessings** – The emotional nourishment and encouragement one person gives another is almost twice as great as the physical nourishment he gives him. Thus, one who gives charity has not yet fulfilled his duty. He must give it with a smile. He must give it with kind words.

[36] **Peace between Me and him** – The pauper in his misery, issues a complaint against Hashem's justice. It is not that he is evil or lacks faith. Rather, his suffering forces his hand and embitters him. When however, others show him sympathy, when they relieve him of his pain, he may again think straight. He may again realize that Hashem is good and kind. Who makes this peace between Hashem and the pauper? – The one who helps him.

Moreover, when a person acts kindly, Hashem also acts kindly, and brings the world closer to perfection. Thus, with his charity, the kind person prompts Hashem to bring healing, peace and prosperity into the world.

[37] **The poor man is closer to the King** – "Hashem is close to those who call to Him with sincerity." (Tehillim 145.18) Accordingly, the pauper can hurt a person more than anyone else. Therefore he must be sensitive to the pauper; he must feel his pain, his shame. He must speak to him gently, respectfully.

R' Yehuda b'Rebbi Shalom taught: Just as Heaven determines a person's livelihood from *Rosh haShana*, so it determines his losses from *Rosh haShana*. If he merits, he gives them to the poor; if not, tax-collectors receive them.[39] (Bava Basra 10a)

Raban Yochanan ben Zakai saw in a dream that his nephews would lose 700 *dinarim* that year. He therefore pressured them throughout the year, to give this amount to charity. They gave all, except for 17 *dinarim*. On *Erev Yom Kippur* the courts of the Caesar confiscated this sum. [The nephews however, were worried that these courts would still oppress them further.]

"Don't fear," Raban Yochanan told them, "they only want 17 *dinarim*."

"How do you know this?" they asked in amazement.

"I saw it in a dream," he told them.

"Why then didn't you tell us; we would rather have it go to charity," they asked.

"I wanted you to give it with pure motivations"[40] he answered. (ibid.)

In R' Yishmael's yeshiva they taught: One who shears his property, using it for charity, saves himself from the punishments of *Gehinom*.

This may be compared to two sheep crossing a river, one that was sheared, and another that was not. Only the sheared one made it to the other side.[41] The unsheared one however, drowned. (Gitin 7b)

---

[38] **With money** – The punishment for a sin or a mitzva not done is death or physical pain, (Yerushalmi, Makkos 2). Money is a completely inadequate substitute. Still, giving charity can change all this. One reason is that since it makes him a better, more spiritual person, a new and different person, he is no longer the guilty party. Furthermore, the pain he suffers when he parts with his money also cleanses him of his sin. Thus, Hashem in His mercy, may free him of the sufferings that were his due.

[39] **Tax-collectors receive them** – The rule is that a sinner does not profit from his sins (Shvi'is 9.9). Thus, one who does not give charity, must lose this money is some other way. He ends up paying it to tax-collectors and traffic officers, if not to doctors, dentists and lawyers.

Still, a person should feel grateful for such losses. For they save him from uglier punishments – the horrible tortures of Gehinom. Even so, the best of options remains to give these funds to charity.

[40] **With pure motivations** – While all mitzvos reach to the Heavens, not all of them enter this heavenly realm. Only the mitzvos a person does with pure intentions have this thrust. Those mitzvos however, that he does with impure motives, must wait at the heavenly gates for their final repair. (Pesachim 50b)

A Wheel of Fortune

There are other reasons why a person may suffer. One is a product of mazal – there is a turning wheel of fortune,[42] bringing one person to wealth, while it brings another to poverty.

"When a poor man comes to the door," Rav Chiya told his wife, "offer him a meal,[43] so that others too will take mercy and feed our children."

"Are you cursing our children?!" she asked.

"No," he answered, "but the Yeshiva of R' Yishmael has already taught that there is a wheel that turns in the world, and one that is affluent today, may well be poor tomorrow." (Shabbos 151b)

Yosi ben Yochanan, a man of Yerushalayim said: Let your house be wide open, and let the poor be a part of your home.[44] (Avos 1.5)

Still...

"There shall be no poor amongst you." (Devarim 15.4)

While a person must toil for his friend's well-being, he should not impoverish himself in the process. His interests come first.[45] (Bava Metzia 30b, Rashi there)

---

[41] **The sheared one made it to the other side** – Giving charity is like shearing a sheep. Just as a shorn sheep does not drown, so too a person shorn of his material possessions escapes Gehinom. (Rashi)

There is a second idea here. This is that just as the wool of the sheared sheep increases at a faster rate, so the person who shears his income also enjoys a greater growth. (See Rashi there)

[42] **A turning wheel of fortune** – Good fortunes visit a family for a time, and then move on to others, allowing them also to enjoy its favors. May one's merits override one's mazal? – See the chapter on Mazal, p.42.

[43] **Offer him a meal** – Even when there is a heavenly decree that a person or his children must suffer poverty, he may sweeten his lot with charity.

[44] **A part of your home** – How may one guarantee that his wealth does not pass over to others, that it does not swing from the rich man to his poor counterpart? The Torah solution is to ensure that the poor share his wealth with him; that they also enjoy the comforts and conveniences he so enjoys. For thus he creates an equality between the rich and the poor – an equality whose benefits he too will one day, enjoy.

Also, when he brings them into his house, making his good fortune their good fortune, their good fortune likewise, becomes his good fortune. When he makes his best interests their best interests, their best interests likewise, become his best interests.

One who scatters his money,[46] should not scatter more than a fifth of his wealth[47] – that he should not come to depend on others. (Kesuvos 50a)

Rabba said: Householders who free their slaves,[48] lose their wealth. (Gitin 38b)

---

[45] **His interests come first** – While a person has a mitzva to concern himself with the welfare of the poor, he certainly does them no favor by joining their ranks and becoming yet another mouth to feed.

[46] **One who scatters** – Before we compared the giving of charity to fertilizer. Here too, this resemblance applies. For like a person spoils his crop with too much fertilizer, similarly he may impoverish himself with excessive generosity.

Still, we may ask, does this not contradict the teaching that the bread a person throws on the waters will eventually return to him? That the charity he gives, will enrich him?

The answer is that a person lives in the present. As such, he must cater for the present needs of himself and his family. If he doesn't do so, he will suffer. For while charity leads to wealth, this however, is a future wealth. Heaven's blessings only comes through normal channels – the mechanics of this 'natural,' physical world. As such, they travel slowly, and a person must await them patiently. He may not rely on miracles to pour riches over him right now.

Moreover, if he allows poverty to overtake him in the present, he may even spoil his chances of receiving future blessings. For in his need, he is like the man with no bucket. Can he catch the rain that falls?!

[47] **No more than a fifth** – There are, however, exceptions to this rule. In these cases our Rabbis permit and even, advise a person to donate more than his fifth. These are:

(1) One who is exceptionally wealthy – giving more than a fifth will not send him into the poorhouse. Likewise, one who is dying does not endanger himself by giving away his wealth. On the contrary, converting his riches into charity, enriches him more than leaving it in this world.

(2) One whose income exceeds his budget. He profits better to spend this money on charitable causes than on luxury items.

(3) One who is approached by a naked, hungry pauper. Once there is an issue of saving a life, a person must be ready to lose all his wealth.

(4) One who supports Torah-learning. Since with this expenditure he acquires a share of the Torah studied for himself, this is not charity in the regular sense. Rather, he should think that just as there are scholars who forfeit lucrative careers to study Torah, so he should feel privileged to 'impoverish' himself for the sake of the Torah. (Ahavas Chesed 2.20)

[48] **Who free their slaves** – There are limits to generosity, and one who crosses these limits, may just accomplish the opposite effect. Freeing a Canaanite slave is seemingly, a generous act. The person who frees his slave, gives him entrance to a normal, independent life. So while there is a financial loss, as with any other

charity, this act should lead to riches. Still, since freeing a slave goes against a direct Torah command, he will enjoy no special merit. The expense of freeing his slave will remain an expense that he must suffer. (Based on Maharsha)

While the laws of slaves are not in effect nowadays, there is still a lesson here. This is that no person may hope for Heaven to bless his endeavors, when he violates Torah law. To enjoy a wealth that carries Heaven's blessings, he must please the Heavens with his deeds.

CHAPTER NINE

HONOR YOUR WIFE

Goodness

It's not enough to do acts of kindness with others, one must act kindly with one's family as well. Who then should the generous man begin with, if not his wife?[1] This is especially important for another reason. She, our Rabbis teach us, is every husband's source of prosperity and happiness.

He who finds a wife, finds goodness; he will receive Hashem's good favor. (Mishle 18.22)

R' Chanilai said: A man who has no wife lives without joy,[2] without blessing[3] and without goodness.[4]

In the West they say: He dwells without Torah[5] and without a wall.[6]

Rava bar Ulla said: He dwells without peace.[7] (Yevamos 62b)

---

[1] **His wife** – While this chapter specifically addresses men, its lesson applies equally to women. For the woman who builds up her husband, who gives him love, esteem and a sense of worth, enjoys a wondrous life. With her input, her support, he builds her a grand castle; as the prophet teaches: "When her husband trusts her with his heart, [their home] will lack no spoils." (Mishle 31.11). Also: "The wisdom of women builds its home." (ibid. 14.1)

[2] **Without joy** – Even if a person lives with every luxury, he will not enjoy it unless he has a companion to share it with him. And who is the companion that best matches him? Who is one that may save him from his loneliness? – Only his wife.

[3] **Without blessing** – Hashem sends a man wealth and other heavenly blessings, through his wife.

[4] **Without goodness** – She fires him to reach for and achieve great goals. It is through her, that he finds success. It is through her, that his life overflows with goodness. (R. David Carno)

[5] **Without Torah** – Only one who learns to be truly sensitive to another, can be sensitive to the subtleties and nuances the Torah contains.

[6] **Without a wall** – Once a person lives without joy, blessing, goodness and Torah, he is vulnerable to the many negative, evil forces that blow through his world.

[7] **Without peace** – The man who lives alone may imagine that he can satisfy his every need. This however, is a mistake. As much as he acquires, he will never acquire serenity; as the verse teaches, "There is no peace, says Hashem, for the selfish-wicked." (Yeshayahu 48.22)

R' Elazar said: A man who has no wife is no man.[8] (Yevamos 63a)

Love and Honor

Rav Chelbo said, "A man should always treat his wife with respect, for blessing only enters his house on her account.[9]

Similarly Rava told the people of Mechuza, "Honor your wives, that you may become rich." (Bava Metzia 59a)

Rav Avira taught, at times in Rav Ami's name, and at times in Rav Assi's name: A person should eat and drink at a level less than he can afford, clothe and acquire a home according to what he can afford[10] and honor his wife and children more than he can afford; for they depend on him,[11] while he depends on the One who created the world with His word. (Chulin 84b)

Rav Yitzchak taught: One who has lived with his wife for a time, even if he becomes poor, she will not reject him. "When he had wealth," she will say, "he fed and clothed me, therefore I will not leave him."

However, a prostitute, when he gives her gifts she is appreciative, but when he doesn't give her gifts, she doesn't know him.[12] (Shmos Raba 32.5)

---

[8] **He is no man** – A man only realizes his strength and potential if he first unites himself in marriage with a woman.

[9] **On her account** – When Avram went down to Egypt, he asked his wife, Sara, to say that she was his sister. Pharaoh, thinking he could marry her, then gave great expensive gifts to Avram; as the verse states, "and he benefited Avram for her sake." (Breishis 12.16)
This our Rabbis tell us, is not an incidental detail of the story; rather it teaches that the wealth a man receives, comes to him through his wife.

[10] **Clothe and acquire a home according to what he can afford** – so that he does not suffer from embarrassment.

[11] **They depend on him** – As he cares for those who depend on him, so will Hashem, on Whom he depends, care for him.

[12] **She doesn't know him** – This is the difference between a wife and a prostitute. If a man has a wife, she stands by him through his difficulties. If however, he marries a prostitute, once problems arise, she deserts him.
Similarly, when a person lives the right type of life – when he has the correct value-system and chooses his friends accordingly – then no problem can destroy him. While he may suffer difficulties, he maintains his life-style and his relations with others. However, when he lives with improper values, when he replaces morality with lustful satisfactions, he too is a 'prostitute.' Like the woman who exploits her husband, so a person who lives only for pleasure, perverts himself. Moreover, he

Warnings

Just as honoring one's wife brings to wealth, so a lack of honor has the opposite effect.

Rav Huna taught: One who is cursed by his wife,[13] comes to poverty.

"Being cursed by his wife," said Rava, "refers to a case where he doesn't buy her jewelry; this however, is only true where he can afford to buy it.[14] (Shabbos 62b)

Rava bar Rav Ada said in the name of Rav: One who marries a woman for her money,[15] will have ill-bred children ...

The *Gemara* asks: Maybe at least, he will enjoy the money?

"No," the *Gemara* answers, "within a month he will squander it all."[16] (Kidushin 70a)

One who hopes for his wife's earnings ... sees no blessing.

This however, refers to one who sends his wife to the market with a scale.[17]

---

gambles away life's every goodness. For if he loses his material wealth, he has nothing to fall back on.

[13] **One who is cursed –** "Can I help it if she curses me?" a husband may ask. The answer is definitely, yes. One person will only curse another is he feels that the other is not fulfilling his duties, he is not doing that which he should be doing.

And if the husband asks, "Is it so terrible that she curses me?" The answer again, is yes. No person can afford to have others curse him, especially his spouse. For a curse contains a terrible power, and may cause a person much evil. Even when others do not curse him openly, but only in their hearts, this too exacts its price. Thus he must be careful not to arouse the resentment of others.

[14] **Where he can afford to buy it –** If a woman feels her husband could be buying her fine clothes and adornments and is not, she may just curse him. Even if she only curses him in her heart, a curse is still a curse. Therefore, he must take care either to buy her pretty items, or alternatively, explain to her that he really wants her to have jewelry, but cannot afford this right now. If he shows her his sincerity, this itself honors her, and brings him prosperity.

[15] **For her money –** This speaks of a lowly woman, one whom such a man should never marry. However, one may marry a good woman who is also rich. Still, even when she is worthy, he should not marry her for her money. Such a motive brings only to anguish. (Rashi)

[16] **He will squander it all –** Hashem does not bless such funds.

[17] **He sends his wife to the market with a scale –** that she may rent it out for a small fee. This is degrading work that earns her little money. (Rashi) This does not mean however, that she need not work at all. On the contrary, the Torah praises

Peace and Harmony

The man who together with honoring his wife, fulfills his duties to his family and society, achieves a harmony and peace that makes for true wealth.

The Rabbis taught: One who loves his wife as himself,[18] and honors her more than himself, who guides his children along the straight path,[19] and marries them when they reach maturity – of him the verse says, "Know that there will be peace in your tent." (Iyov 5.24). (Yevamos 62b)

The Rabbis taught: One who loves his neighbors and helps his relatives, who marries off his niece and lends money to a man in distress – of him the verse says, "Then you will call, and Hashem will answer;[20] you will cry out, and He will respond... (Yeshayahu 58.9)" (Yevamos 62b)

Women too

While this chapter speaks to men, most of what it says applies equally to women. For the woman who builds up her husband, who gives him love, esteem and a sense of worth, enjoys a wondrous life. With her input, her support, she builds a grand palace of a home; as the verse teaches:

"The wisdom of the woman builds her home." (Mishle 14.1)

Also, she wins the trust of her husband, which brings still more riches into their home:

---

the woman who makes her own goods and sells them. Thus the verse states: "She makes cloth, and sells it" (Mishle 31). (Pesachim 50b)

The rule is that a husband must carefully honor his wife in many different ways. If he needs her to work, he must ensure that she has an honorable craft, and does not engage in anything that cheapens her. Only that which enhances her honor, will bring them blessings.

[18] **One who loves his wife as himself** – Loving one's wife, means giving her of his own, making sacrifices for her. Such acts of giving draw him nearer to her, and her to him. Whether she learns of these gifts or not, is unimportant. The main thing is that he gives to her. (See Michtav M'Eliyahu, Kuntras haChesed)

[19] **Who guides his children along the straight path** – Many people do not discipline their children for fear that it will lead to a lack of harmony and friendship. Here we learn that the exact opposite is true. It is specifically by guiding them properly, that a person enjoys peace in his home.

[20] **Hashem will answer** – When a person is kind to his relatives and neighbors, when he cares for them as he cares for his own, he merits special heavenly aid.

"When her husband trusts her with his heart, [their home] lacks no spoils."[21] (Mishle 31.11)

---

[21] A woman once went to her lawyer to ask for his help in arranging a divorce.
"Also" she told the lawyer, "I want to take revenge for the many wrongs he inflicted on me."
"In that case," answered the lawyer, "go back home, be the best possible wife you can be for the next few months, and then leave him. This surely will give him the biggest slap in the face."
The woman followed her lawyer's advice. However, after these months were over, she decided that she wanted to stay married to him after all. (Heard from Mrs. Tova Vodislovski)

CHAPTER TEN
GREAT PEOPLE II

Leadership

A person who gives to others is naturally called on to accept leadership. As a giver, others elevate him to levels where his influence may spread further and further. This influence in turn, brings him still greater prosperity, and other gifts.

Once a person becomes a communal leader, he becomes wealthy.[1] (Yoma 22b)

R' Yirmiah taught: A community leader must be *wealthy*, [for to lead effectively] he must have none above him besides Hashem.[2] (Horios 9a)

R' Yochanan said: The Divine Presence rests only on one who is wise, strong, rich and humble – the qualities of our teacher, Moshe. (Nedarim 38a)

R' Yochanan said: All the prophets were rich men.[3] (ibid.)

---

[1] **He becomes wealthy** – Why wealth? – A leader needs forcefulness to enact and carry through his task. Thus he needs wisdom, charisma, power and also wealth. He needs wealth to influence those people who are impressed by elegant garments, mighty limousines, handsome homes, etc.

He becomes wealthy – The Rabbis do not speak here of leadership positions that carry large salaries. Such jobs obviously enrich a person. Rather, they refer to positions that do not carry handsome rewards; even such positions make a person wealthy!

While leadership attracts many people with the prestige it offers, there is a more important reason for accepting this responsibility. This is the kindness the job entails. For a community leader works for the good of the community – he helps his community live fuller, richer lives. This is good for the community, and for Hashem. In turn, the good and caring leader receives large helpings of heavenly kindness. Hashem grants him all he may need to effectively fulfill his task, and so, he prospers greatly.

[2] **None above him** – He must have the freedom to act as he feels is best.

[3] **All the prophets were rich men** – The prophets are agents of Hashem; He assigned them to direct His people in His holy ways. Therefore he gave them qualities that people admire; attributes that will help them to influence the public. (Ibn Tevon, quoted by Maharsha)

"...your exalted power."[4] (VaYikra 26.19) What does the verse refer to?

Rav Yosef taught: This refers to the wealthy men of Yehuda. (Gitin 37a)

Responsibilities

Hashem however, does not give a person the quality of leadership, that he may gain greater wealth and honor. These are side-benefits. The essential element of leadership, is accepting responsibility.

"You should know," R' Yehoshua once told Raban Gamliel, "that you have two students who know how to calculate how many drops there are in the sea, yet they have neither bread to eat, nor a garment to wear!"

Raban Gamliel thereon decided to give them positions of authority [that would entitle them to draw salaries]. He sent for them, but they did not come. Again he sent for them; this time they came.

"Do you think I am giving you lordship [that you so piously reject my offer," he asked, "know, that it is not lordship I give you;] it is servitude[5] I give you ..." (Horios 10a)

Today our spiritual leaders stand in the place of prophets. And who appoints our spiritual leaders? – The answer is nobody. Anyone who wishes to benefit the public; may do so. From the above teaching we learn if a person does volunteer his leadership qualities, and his intentions please Hashem, he may well hope to merit wisdom, strength, wealth and humility, as well as a special heavenly help.

[4] **Your exalted power** – At the simplest level, the verse speaks of the Beis haMikdash, the holy Temple (Rashi). At a deeper level though, it refers to the wealthy. The question is, can we really compare the two?

The aim of the Beis haMikdash is to focus the eyes of the Jewish people on the service of Hashem. It is a construction of glory, and as such, fills the people with pride; it inspires them to reach ever-higher levels.

Similarly, the wealthy serve as a focal point. People admire them from a distance, and look to them as role models. This is the reality of their social position, a part of the power their wealth automatically gives them.

If they use this influence properly, their wealth will increase. Moreover, their heavenly rewards will multiply repeatedly. For since they move the multitudes closer to Hashem, they have the greatest merit of all. It is for such a merit that the great kings, Shaul (Saul) and David strove with each other (Rav Avigdor Miller); and it is such a merit that every great person should strive to attain.

[5] **Servitude** – One who leads the people is a servant to the people. This, however, does not debase him. On the contrary, the more he lowers himself, the more Hashem elevates him. (From the Ramban's letter)

On his Head

Just as leadership leads to wealth, wealth leads to leadership. A person who is wealthy must take on responsibility for those who are less fortunate than himself. He must teach and lead people along righteous paths. If he fails to do so, he jeopardizes his wealth. Moreover, the blame for their sins falls painfully on his head.

The Mishna states that R' Elazar ben Azarya's cow carried a ribbon on its horns on Shabbos, against the wishes of the Rabbis.

The Gemara asks: Did R' Elazar ben Azarya have only one cow; surely Rav (and some say Rav Yehuda), taught that his yearly tithe was twelve thousand calves?[6]

It was really his neighbor's cow, the Gemara answers, still since he did not object to her behavior, they called it by his name.[7] (Shabbos 54a)

The wealth of those who are able to rebuke others and don't do so, is confiscated. (Sukka 29a)

Rav said: The wealth of those who avoid their responsibilities and duties, passing them on to someone else, declines and disappears. (ibid. 29b)

People hate the rich man who denies his debts and duties.[8] (Pesachim 113b)

---

[6] **His yearly tithe was twelve thousand calves** – This means that his herds were producing 120 000 new calves every year!

[7] **By his name** – A person with wealth and influence is responsible for others. Thus the Gemara labels the cow that belonged to Rebbi Elazar's neighbor, his. For the obligation to keep his neighbor from breaking Shabbos belonged not only to this simple woman, but to the learned, influential scholar who was her neighbor. Likewise, every person with wealth and power, must recognize his effect on others – his ability to educate and direct them – and then act accordingly.

[8] **Who denies his debts and duties** – A person must live in peace and harmony; otherwise, he cannot achieve true prosperity. Before the community will accept the rich man as a leader, he must carry some of the community's burden. For once he has wealth, he has an ability to help others. Accordingly, people view him as a source of salvation. He in turn, must live up to their expectations, and honor their respect. If, however, he avoids his duties, he arouses the public's enmity. This leads neither to his well-being, nor to any other benefits. On the contrary, it ultimately, ruins him.

From our Rabbis

The effects of good leadership are so important, that our Rabbis went to great lengths to encourage people of ability and influence to accept the yoke of the community.

R' Yehuda HaNasi showed honor to the wealthy.[9] R' Akiva showed honor to the wealthy. Why? For the world dwells in peace before Hashem,[10] only when the wealthy give food and shelter to the poor. (Eiruvim 86a)

How?

Sometimes a person thinks, what can I do for others? He sees an affluent environment: "Everyone is rich here; I cannot achieve anything!" Or more frequently, the opposite is the problem. He throws his hands up: "Everyone here is poor; who can help who?" Therefore our Rabbis inform us:

No community is either fully rich, or fully poor.[11] (Yerushalmi Gitin 3.7.)

We must carry out our duties, and to the fullest degree...

The Rabbis taught: We feed the non-Jewish poor alongside with the Jewish poor; We visit the non-Jewish sick alongside with the Jewish sick,

---

[9] **R' Yehuda HaNasi showed honor to the wealthy** – While great Torah scholars prefer always to give honor and glory to spiritual pursuits, they also honor the rich. For by showing extra love and respect to those who possess wealth and influence, they encourage them to help others, and draw them closer to spiritual pursuits.

[10] **The world dwells in peace** – "Kindness builds the world" (Tehillim 33.5) Where there is kindness, there the world prospers. Once people help each other, support each other, smile at each other, the community thrives and flourishes. Hashem blesses their endeavors and efforts, and they enjoy prosperity and affluence. Moreover, Hashem moves the world closer to its final redemption.

Here then is a good reason to acquire wealth. It is to help the community, and build up the world. A person who aspires to wealth, should see this as his motive. Then, he will merit that others admire and love him, that they bless his goals, and help him achieve great success.

[11] **Fully rich, or fully poor** – There are always those who need help; and there are always those who can help. Therefore, no individual should think, "Who am I?" or "What can I do?" If he gives his thoughts to benefitting others, Hashem will send him both the financial means and the insight to do just this!

we bury the non-Jewish poor together with Jewish poor.[12] Why? For the [Torah's ways are] ways of peace. (Gitin 61a)

---

[12] **Alongside with the Jewish poor** – Community care is no simple task. We must learn to help others, and help them generously. At the same time however, we may not waste precious resources. We must allocate finances and personnel in an optimum way.

Still, we cannot be too clever. While certain charities seem contrary to the community's interests, for example, helping and supporting the non-Jewish poor, we must nevertheless lend a hand. For peace is vital to a Torah life-style, and we must pursue it. What of the expense this will involve? – Once Hashem desires us to act like this, we should trust that He will compensate us for our expenses, and reward us for our efforts.

CHAPTER ELEVEN
SHABBOS

A Special Device

Logically, keeping Shabbos should only impoverish a person. He loses a whole work-day, a day where he could be earning. This is reasonable. This makes sense. Still, the truth is the exact opposite.

The Roman government once decreed that the Jews should not keep Shabbos. R' Reuven ben Isteroboli went, shaved his forehead [that he might look like a Roman], and sat with them.

"One who has an enemy," he asked them, "should he make him poor or rich?"

"He should make him poor," they all answered.

"If so, let the Jews cease from working on Shabbos, that they may be poor" he told them.

"Well said," they replied, "we will annul the decree," and they annulled it.

However, when they discovered later that Reb Reuven was a Jew, they instituted it again.[1] (Me'ila 17a)

Expense Account

There are a number of ways Shabbos helps a person towards wealth. The first is by compensating him for all that he spends in the honor of Shabbos.

Rav Tachlipha, brother of Ravnai Chozah, taught: A person's livelihood is fixed from Rosh haShana to Rosh haShana, with the exception of what he spends on Shabbos and Yom Tov ...[2] If he cuts back his expenses on them, the Heavens correspondingly cut back on his allowance; and if he spends more[3] on them, they correspondingly, increase it. (Beitza 16a)

---

[1] **They renewed their decree** – Even the Romans could understand that Shabbos is a source of blessing for the Jewish people.

[2] **What he spends on Shabbos and Yom Tov** – as well as what he spends on his children's Torah education. (ibid.)

[3] **If he spends more** – He must be careful though, to direct his expenses towards glorifying the Shabbos, and not just honoring his stomach.

A Source of Wealth

However, beyond the fact that Shabbos does not burden a person financially, it also brings him wealth.

"Rebbi," asked R' Yishmael b'Rebbi Yosi, "How do the wealthy of *Bavel* merit their wealth?"

"Through honoring the Torah," he answered.

"And in other lands?" R' asked.

"Through honoring the Shabbos."[4] (Shabbos 119a)

R' Yochanan said in the name of R' Yosi: One who gives delight to the Shabbos,[5] receives an inheritance that has no boundaries...

Rav Yehuda said in the name of Rav: One who gives delight to the Shabbos, receives his heart's desires. (Shabbos 118a,b)

R' Chiya bar Aba related, "Once a certain man in Ludkia hosted me. The servants brought in a golden table so heavy, that sixteen men had to carry it. Silver chains were fixed to it. Bowls and cups, jugs and flasks adorned it. Every type of food, delicacy and spice graced it.

As they set it down they proclaimed, "The earth and its contents belongs to Hashem." (Tehillim 24.1)

When they removed it they declared, "The Heavens are Hashem's, while the earth he gave to man." (Tehillim 115.16)

How did you merit this wealth, my son?" I asked him.

"I was a butcher," he told me, "and whenever a beautiful animal came my way,[6] I would set it aside for Shabbos."

---

[4] **Through honoring the Shabbos** – The person who honors and glorifies Hashem brings blessing and prosperity into his world. Thus, for example, when he honors Torah scholars, this is a form of honoring Hashem, and it brings him wealth.

What of those lands where there are no Torah scholars? How may he gain this merit there? This is through honoring Shabbos. By showing honor to this holy day, he testifies to the belief that Hashem created the world, and completely controls it. Thus, he honors his Master.

Every Jew must keep Shabbos. If he doesn't do so, the Torah discounts his status as a Jew. On the other hand, when he not only keeps the Shabbos but also honors her, he is a Jew in the best possible sense – and he merits the greatest of heavenly blessings.

[5] **One who gives delight to the Shabbos** – The essential mitzva is to treat the Shabbos queen as an important guest; to honor her with tasty meals, a tidy home and festive behavior. (Heard from Rav Shmuel Yitzchok Herman)

"How fortunate you are," I told him, "that you merited so much, and blessed is Hashem who gave you all this." (Shabbos 119a)

A Generous Employer

Once, there was a certain very wealthy non-Jew who lived near Yosef Mokir-Shabsa, (Yosef who honored Shabbos). Star-gazers told him, "We see that Yosef Mokir-Shabsa has eaten all your wealth."[7]

On hearing this the non-Jew went, sold all his property, and bought a precious jewel with the proceeds. He hid the jewel in his hat.[8]

Once when he crossed a bridge, the wind blew his hat into the river. A fish swallowed the jewel. Fishermen caught the fish on Erev Shabbos.

"Who will buy this fish now?" they asked.

"Take it to Yosef Mokir-Shabsa," they told them, "who usually buys delicacies in honor of Shabbos." Yosef bought it, tore it open, and found the jewel. He sold it for thirteen attics of golden *dinarim*.

An old man met Yosef and told him; "One who lends to Shabbos,[9] Shabbos repays him!" (Shabbos 119a)

---

[6] **A beautiful animal** – He would reserve only the best of meat. However, of greater importance, he would do this specifically, for Shabbos's honor.

[7] **Yosef Mokir-Shabsa has eaten all your wealth** – Yosef spent so much on Shabbos, that he had already consumed the equivalent of the non-Jew's wealth in the honor of Shabbos. (Maharsha)

[8] **He hid the jewel** – While the non-Jew may well have realized that all his wealth only existed for the honor of Hashem, and therefore belonged to the Jew who served Hashem, nevertheless he tried to prevent him from receiving his wealth. His plan however, not only did not help him, it even simplified the process by which Yosef would receive his wealth.

[9] **One who lends to Shabbos** – How could Yosef have 'lent' so much money to Shabbos? While 'the thirteen attics of gold coins' mentioned is an exaggeration (Rashi), still it does indicate that Yosef received a fortune – after all, this non-Jew was a wealthy man!

We must say therefore, that Shabbos repaid him not only for his expenses, but also for all the effort he exerted to honor Shabbos, the ingenuity he displayed to promote her beauty. These efforts demand that he receive a beautiful compensation.

Perks

The Rabbis taught: There is a hard-worker who profits, and a hard-worker who loses; [likewise] there is a lazy-worker who profits and a lazy-worker who loses.

There is a hard-worker who profits – this is the person who works all week and does not work on *Erev Shabbos*. There is a hard-worker who loses – this is the person who works all week, and also works on *Erev Shabbos*.[10]

There is lazy-worker who profits – This is a person who doesn't work all week, and also doesn't work on *Erev Shabbos*.[11] There is a lazy-worker who loses – This is a person who doesn't work all week, but *does* work on *Erev Shabbos*. (Pesachim 50b)

For her Honor

There was a wealthy family in Yerushalayim. But because they feasted on Erev Shabbos, [thus entering Shabbos with full stomachs and shaming her honor], they lost their wealth. (Gitin 38b)

---

[10] **He works on Erev Shabbos –** Hard work alone does not lead to prosperity. Every person needs Hashem to bless his endeavors. For without this blessing his attempts are in vain, the fruits of his labors may simply all rot. On the other hand, with Hashem's blessing, even the most pathetic attempts may develop into treasure-chests of riches. With Hashem's blessing, even 'the lazy worker' may prosper.

Shabbos is our great source of blessing, prosperity and well-being. On Shabbos we stop all week-day activity, and rest. This rest allows us to realize that Hashem owns all, that He controls all. Moreover, when we honor Shabbos – really honor her – we draw closer to our Maker, and merit Hashem's friendship, and blessing.

A great element of honoring Shabbos is devoting time to its preparations. The more a person invests in preparing himself, the more successful his Shabbos is. This is true not only in the physical sense. With his preparations he trains himself to appreciate Shabbos to an ever-greater, ever-deeper extent.

The most important time to prepare for Shabbos is Erev Shabbos. Here a person may give his whole self to her honor. Ceasing from work alone already gives honor to Shabbos; how much the more so, if he uses this time to prepare treats for the Shabbos. Then he truly merits her blessings.

[11] **He also doesn't work on Erev Shabbos –** The fact that he doesn't work all week long, does not withhold him from enjoying the brocha of not working on Erev Shabbos.

Rabba said: Householders who inspect their property on Shabbos,[12] lose their wealth. (Gitin 38b)

A certain pious man once walked in his vineyard on Shabbos thinking all along how he might improve it. Suddenly he found a hole in his fence.

"I will not fix this hole," he rebuked himself, "for I had thought to fix it on Shabbos!"

What then did Hashem then do? He sent a caper-bush that sealed his wall. Moreover, the bush sustained the pious man with its fruits for the rest of his life. (VaYikra Raba 34.16)

We should not even pray for our personal needs on Shabbos...

"How then do we pray in the Birkas haMazon, 'feed us, sustain us'?"[13] R' Zeira asked R' Chiya bar Aba.

"This is the format of the blessing,"[14] he answered. (ibid.)

Another Shabbos

Just as the seven-day week has the Shabbos day as its crown, so the seven-year cycle has its special Shabbos, the Shmitta year. And just as observing the Shabbos day brings him to prosperity, while scorning it leads to poverty, similarly and even more so, observing Shmitta brings him to riches,[15] while profaning it leads to his downfall.

---

[12] **Householders who inspect their property** – On Shabbos a person trains himself to think that it is only Hashem who truly produces and creates; he focuses on the thought that it is only Hashem who cares for his needs. How so? – By not doing any work himself. However, when he inspects his property or engages in some other weekday pursuit on this holy day, he spoils the lesson of Shabbos; he tarnishes its beauty.

The work a person does during the week, receives its blessing from Shabbos. It receives a blessing when he understands – in the deepest, most profound of ways – that it is only Hashem who sustains him. However when he violates Shabbos, he forfeits this blessing. This leads him to poverty. (Based on the Maharsha)

[13] **Feed us, sustain us** – We do not pray for our personal needs on Shabbos, for this is the day we must understand, that only Hashem cares for our needs – even when we do not prompt Him.

[14] **This is the format of the blessing** – and a person does not think of his problems when he recites it. (Rav Ze'ev Wolf Einhorn)

[15] **Even more so, observing** Shmitta **brings him riches** – If not working one day a week teaches us that Hashem runs all, how much the more then does not working for a full year, show us that Hashem controls the world.

Hashem cherishes "the sevens"[16]... Amongst the days, the seventh day is dearer than all other days. Amongst the years, the seventh year is dearer than all other years. (VaYikra Raba 29.11)

When *Yisrael* fulfills Hashem's wish they keep *Shmitta* once in seven years, but when they do not fulfill His will, they must keep four *Shmittas* in seven years.

How so? To produce good crops, a farmer leaves his field fallow one year and farms it the next. Thus he leaves his field fallow four times in seven years; but if he keeps *Shmitta*, Hashem blesses his field and he need only leave the field fallow once in seven years.[17] (Mechilta Mishpatim 23.213)

"Warn *Yisrael* to keep *Shmitta*," Hashem told Moshe, "so that they are not exiled from the land."[18] (Yalkut Shimoni, BeHar 658.)

A person eager to become rich who does not keep *Shmitta*, thinks that this will help him. Hashem however, tells him: "You will lose through this; you have cursed your own property, and now you will have to sell it."[19] (Tanchuma BeHar 1)

------

[16] **"The sevens"** – Other sevens Hashem endears include: the seventh Heaven, Arvos; the tzaddik of the seventh generation from Creation, Chanoch; the seventh leader of the Jewish people, Moshe; the seventh Jewish king, Asa; the year that culminates the seventh of the seven-year cycles, Yoveil – the Jubilee year; the seventh month of the year, Tishrei.

[17] **Once in seven years** – Many of the Torah's mitzvos appear at first to add discomfort and inconvenience to our lives. However, the riches that come in their wake more than compensate us for our troubles. Thus, the farmer who must cease farming, may at first cry over his financial losses; but eventually, he will realize that he is only the richer for them.

[18] **So that they are not exiled** – This is the special punishment for those who disregard the Shmitta. For only when they are off the land may the land then 'catch up' on the spiritual rest that the people had denied it.

[19] **You will have to sell it** – When we misuse the gifts Hashem gives us, we must, against our will, forfeit them.

R' Yosi b'Rebbi Chanina taught: See how severe is the dust of *Shmitta*[20] – if a person buys and sells seventh year fruits, Heaven impoverishes him such that he must sell up his goods. If he is indifferent to Heaven's message and does not change his ways, they force him to sell his fields. If he is indifferent to this message and does not change his ways, they force him to sell his house. If he is indifferent to this message and does not change his ways, they force him to sell his daughter as a maidservant. If he is indifferent to this message and does not change his ways, they force him borrow money with *ribis*. If he is indifferent to this message and does not change his ways, they force him sell himself. (Kidushin 20a)

---

[20] **The dust of** Shmitta – These are rules that only border on the actual prohibitions of Shmitta, and are not Torah requirements themselves. Dealing with Shmitta produce is just such a sin, and one of the lightest of those relating to Shmitta. For this reason the Rabbis call it "dust." Still it carries a harsh punishment. As a result of it, Heaven forces his financial downfall, and he must sell his property.

While this message may be a subtle one, still, one who wishes to understand, understands it very clearly. Moreover, if he takes the lesson to heart and repents, Hashem will restore to him all He took. (Rashi) However, if he disregards this message, he is punished further and further. As his sin brings him lower, so his punishment grows increasingly harsh. It enwraps and chokes him in its grip, until he breaks. For only thus may he, and those who follow him, attach importance to Hashem's word.

There is an important idea regarding wealth, that comes directly from the mitzva of Shmitta. This is the idea of 'relative wealth.' The Torah speaks out the objection a person might have to keeping the Shmitta, and offers a unique solution.

'And if you will ask what will we eat in the seventh year when we don't sow or gather in our grain; [Know, says Hashem,] I will command...that the sixth year should produce enough grain for three years, [the sixth, seventh and eighth]. VaYikra 25.20,21.

We see here something interesting. This is that the promise of a triple crop is made only to those who ask what will we eat in the seventh year. No such promise is made to those who don't ask what will we eat in the seventh year. Will they not receive three times the amount of grain? – To answer this question our Rabbis teach that the person who does not ask, does not in fact, receive three times as much grain. Rather he receives the same crop as any other year. Instead, there is a blessing in his food, and the little he has, lasts for three years. What is his gain? – He need not toil and sweat like the farmer with the triple crop. (Rav Leibush Charif, quoted in Mayana shel Torah)

Similarly, there are those that have little wealth, and yet enjoy every one of life's pleasures. How so? With Hashem's blessing. For once they have Hashem's backing, their 'little' goes a very long way.

CHAPTER TWELVE

LOOKING UPWARDS

Trust

Only one who recognizes that Hashem is all-powerful and all-kind, really trusts in Him. For when he knows that Hashem is all-powerful, he understands that Hashem *can* care for him. And when he recognizes that Hashem is all-kind, He sees how Hashem *does* care for him!

Then, once he invests his trust in Hashem, Hashem in return, will send him His all-powerful, all-loving care.

Hashem is my shepherd, [therefore] I lack for nothing; He sets me in lush pastures; He leads me besides tranquil waters. (Tehillim 23.1,2)

Rav Ami said: Anyone who trusts in Hashem, Hashem shields him in this world and in the world-to-come. (Menachos 29b)

Kindness envelops one who trusts in Hashem.[1] (Tehillim 32.10)

Hashem, Lord of Hosts, happy is the person who trusts in you. (Tehillim 84.13)

It is better to trust in Hashem than to trust in man; it is better to trust in Hashem, than to trust [even] in the most generous of men. (Tehillim 118.8,9)

Don't trust in even the most generous man[2] – [for] man does not have the power to save. (Tehillim 146.3)

If Hashem does not build a house, in vain its builders toil; if Hashem will not guard the city, in vain the watchman keeps his watch.[3] (Tehillim 127.1)

The main Torah principle is: *"A righteous person lives by his faith."*[4] *(Chavakuk 2.5)* (Makos 24a)

---

[1] **Kindness envelops one who trusts in Hashem** – It protects him from harm, and surrounds him with goodness.

[2] **In the most generous of men** – Even when you are certain that they care for you, that they have your best interests in mind, still do not trust in them. For their power to help you is limited. They are mortal and weak, and ultimately, in need of help themselves.

[3] **In vain** – Only Hashem is our Builder. Only Hashem is our Protector.

Throw your all on Hashem; He will support you. (Tehillim 55.23)

Hashem sends his blessing through one who has faith.[5] (Shmos Raba 51)

The rain only falls for those who trust in Hashem. (Taanis 8a)

Prayer

One of the most important tools of faith is prayer;[6] its power cannot be emphasized enough. Through prayer a person actualizes his faith. As such it brings him closer to prosperity and happiness.

Rav Yitzchak taught: In these times when the people have neither king, nor prophet, neither *Kohen*, nor *Urim v'Tumim*,[7] they must depend on their prayers alone.[8] (VaYikra Raba 30.3)

R' Yehuda bar Shalom taught in Rebbi Elazar's name: When the rich man speaks, people listen; when the pauper speaks, no one is interested. Hashem however, listens to all who pray to Him.[9] (Shmos Raba 21.4)

---

[4] **By his faith** – The whole world lives by this principle. For within this short phrase, lies the entire essence of the Torah. And it is only for the person who keeps the Torah, that the world continues to run.

[5] **Through one who has faith** – One who trusts in Hashem not only benefits himself – others also gain from his good faith.

[6] **Prayer** – One should pray for all his needs, even for prosperity. Moreover, even when he prays for such a wealth, he should do so with energy, with fervor and with heart. Still, he must be careful that such an ambition does not ruin him; he should pray only for those riches that will allow him to serve Hashem in better, more beautiful ways.

[7] **Urim v'Tumim** – The holy name hidden with the folds of the Kohen Gadol's breast plate. *(Shmos 28.30)* This allowed the Jewish people to receive prophecy from Hashem.

[8] **They must depend on their prayers alone** – And while the power of prayer also decreased with the destruction of the Temple, as we learn...

> *Rebbi Elazar said: From the day the Beis haMikdash was destroyed, a steel wall interrupts between Yisrael and their heavenly Father. (Shabbos 10a)*

Still, the same Rebbi Elazar teaches us that with real effort – with an effort that brings a person to tears – his prayers may yet move worlds.

> *Rebbi Elazar said: Although the gates of prayer are locked, the gates of tears are still open. (ibid.)*

We must learn therefore to cry to Hashem.

[9] **Hashem listens to all** – It is sincerity, trust and hope that impresses Hashem, and not great wealth.

R' Eliezer taught: Know that prayer is powerful – if it doesn't fulfill all one's desires, it at least fulfills half of them.[10] (Devarim Raba 8.1)

Rava saw Rav Hamenuna praying at length.

"Such people desert the world-to-come for this world,"[11] he commented. (Shabbos 10a)

Conditions

R' Meir taught: Why is it that two similar people may pray, yet the one is saved, while the other is not? The one receives his request, while the other does not?

The reason is the one prayed a full prayer,[12] while the other did not. (Rosh haShana 18a)

Abba Shaul said: If a person prays with intent, he can be sure that his prayers will be answered.[13] (Devarim Raba 2.1)

There is a prayer that receives a response in forty days. There is a prayer that receives a response in twenty days. There is a prayer that receives a response in three days. There is a prayer that receives a response in one day. And there is a prayer that receives a response even before the person utters it.[14] (Devarim Raba 2.10)

---

[10] **Half of them** – It is therefore a good practice to ask and to ask, to beg and to pray, at least for twice as much as he needs!

[11] **Such people desert the world-to-come** – Rava agrees that prayer is of the utmost importance; he also agrees that it is fundamental element in building one's world-to-come, as Rebbi Yochanan teaches: *'A person eats the fruits of deep prayer in this world, while the main reward awaits him in the next world.'* (Shabbos 127a) Still, he feels that there is a time for prayer, and a time for learning Torah; and that the one should not be at the expense of the other.

Behind Rava's disapproval, is an important lesson. This is that prayer directly influences a person's prosperity. It affects his health, wealth and peace of mind in this world, along with his spiritual station in the next.

[12] **A full prayer** – The level of the person's concentration is what fills out his prayer and gives it power. *(Rashi)* Thus, the first rule of prayer is to pray with intent.

[13] **His prayers will be answered** – Intent is a matter of degree, the more intense the prayer, the better chance it has of working.

[14] **Even before the person utters it** – What is the magical approach that makes the difference? – Only attitude. First a person must realize that his salvation comes only from Hashem. After all, were it not for Hashem, he would not even know what to ask for. Then, once he realizes this, he will approach his Lord humbly, and with a broken heart. With this approach, he is sure to please Hashem.

Rav Huna bar Brachya said in the name of Rebbi Elazar haKapar: When a person in trouble unites himself with Heaven, Heaven doubles his livelihood.[15] (Brochos 63a)

In shul, on time

R' Yochanan taught in R' Shimon's name: When is it a time of heavenly goodwill? – When the congregation prays.[16] (Brochos 8a)

R' Yochanan taught in R' Shimon's name: When one sets a place for his prayer,[17] his enemies fall before him. (Brochos 7b)

Persistence

Yet another important rule is to keep praying, over and over, until every detail of every request is completely fulfilled!

The needy will not always be forgotten, nor will the hope of the poor be ignored forever.[18] (Tehillim 9.19)

R' Chama b'Rebbi Chanina said: If a person prays and sees that he is not answered, he should pray again. (Brochos 32b)

If the clouds are filled with rains, they must spill them out onto the earth.[19] (Koheles 11.3)

---

[15] **Heaven doubles his livelihood** – *"He unites himself with the Heavens"* means that the person recognizes and blesses Hashem as being "the True Judge" – despite his agony and pain. *(Rashi)*

Also: *"He unites himself with the Heavens"* means that he uses his suffering, as a tool to draw even closer to Hashem. In this way, the person includes Hashem in his daily life, and makes Hashem, *his Partner*. In return, Hashem makes him, His partner, and gives him additional access to His resources. *(Maharsha)*

[16] **When the congregation prays** – A community can accomplish much more than an individual. For when they pray together, they sanctify Hashem's name to a greater degree; they raise it to an even higher Heaven. Thus, *each* individual only profits, by merging his efforts with those of the group.

[17] **When one sets a place for his prayer** – Every time he prays in the same place, he adds the power of *all his previous prayers* to his present requests. This gives his prayer a new power.

[18] **The hope of the poor** – Even when a person's prayers are poor in quality and quantity, still with time and persistent effort, their power will increase. They will affect all that he might wish for.

[19] **They must spill them out** – Just as clouds heavy with water *must* release their rain, so one who loads the Heavens with many steady pleas, must eventually enjoy

Pure Deeds

Observing *mitzvos* and learning Torah bring us closer to Hashem; and the closer we are to Hashem, the more effective are our prayers.

R' Yehoshua of Sichnin said in the name of R' Levi: "If you listen to My commands," Hashem says, "I will listen to your prayers." (Devarim Raba 7.3)

Rav Idi bar Avin said in the name of Rav Yitzchak bar Ashian: If a person prays *and then* goes out to his business, Hashem fulfills his desires. (Brochos 14a)

One who is not deceitful in his business, *merits* to pray a pure prayer. (Shmos 22.4)

On the other hand...

R' Yehoshua haKohen b'Rebbi Nechemia taught: When one soils his hands with theft, Hashem does not answer his prayers. (ibid.)

Seek Him

Rav Ami taught: If one prays, but receives no response, he should go to the pious man of his generation, and ask that he pray to Hashem for him.[20] (Taanis 8a)

R' Yitzchak taught: Why is prayer called 'atar,' meaning 'pitchfork'? The reason is that as a pitchfork turns over grain,[21] so the prayer of the *tzaddik* turns Hashem's conduct from the attribute of strict justice, to one of mercy. (Sukka 14a)

---

their fruits. Their weight will crack open the Heavens, and rain on him their rich blessings.

[20] **That he pray to Hashem for him** – One who understands that he needs Hashem, makes every effort to appease him, even if this means asking someone else to pray for him. Therefore he searches for the best possible advocate to plea-bargain for him. This can only be the pious man of his generation.

[21] **A pitchfork** – How does the *tzaddik* merit a prayer that is like a pitchfork? – We may say that a *tzaddik* is one who conquers and "turns over" his natural drives to fulfill Hashem's will. Accordingly – measure for measure – Hashem 'turns over' His heavenly decrees. He abandons the approach of harsh justice, and adopts instead, an attitude of sweet compassion.

Misplaced Prayers

Heartfelt prayer, recited with holiness, has a power to change nature, making poor the rich, and rich the poor. Still, one must be careful what he asks for...

R' Mani was a student of R' Yitzchak ben Eliyashiv. Once, he came crying to his rebbi.

"The rich members of my father-in-law's house," he complained, "trouble and afflict me."

"May they become poor," R' Yitzchak told him. A while later, he again came to complain before R' Yitzchak.

"Now, there are pressuring me to support them," he cried, "they tell me they have nothing to eat." [22]

"May they become rich," R' Yitzchak prayed, and so it was. (Taanis 23b)

False Trust

Rav Chanin said in the name of Rav Chanina: All who pray *at length*, [while they may not receive all they desire, still] their requests do not return empty-handed.

"Can this be?" asks the Gemara, "surely R' Chiya bar Abba said in the name of R' Yochanan: All who pray *at length*, counting on the prayers for their salvation, come to heartache."

"There is no contradiction," answers the Gemara, "the one teaching speaks of praying at length, and expecting his prayers to save him;[23]

---

[22]**May they be rich** – R' Mani thought he could solve all of his problems with R' Yitzchok's marvelous power of prayer. He learnt though, that it is better sometimes, to let things be.

The *Gemara* relates a similar incident ...

At another time R' Mani came before R' Yitzchak.

"My wife is unattractive," he complained, "and I find it difficult to look at her."

"What is her name?" R' Yitzchak asked.

"Chana"

"May Chana become beautiful," R' Yitzchak prayed, and so it was.

A short while later, R' Mani again came with the complaint.

"She is beautiful now," he cried, "and treats me in an arrogant and offhand way."

"If so," R' Yitzchak said, "May she again be plain." And so it was. (Taanis 23b)

[23] **Expecting his prayers to save him** – They wait and hope for something that *never* comes. (Rashi) A person may not invest his trust *into* his prayers – to feel that

while the other teaching speaks of one praying at length, without expecting his prayers to save him. (Shabbos 10a)

Prayer and Effort

Though no person may cease from toiling over his livelihood [as the Torah decrees, *"With the sweat of your brow, you shall eat bread" (Breishis 3.19),*] ultimately though, he must look only to the One who daily feeds, heals, and gets him through his every day.

"What should a person do to become rich?" The people of Alexandria asked R' Yehoshua ben Chananya.

"Let him engage in much business, buying and selling with honesty," R' Yehoshua answered.

"Many have acted thus," they retorted, "and it didn't help them!"

"Let him then pray to the One who is the Master of all wealth, as the verse says, *'Mine is the silver; Mine is the gold...' (Chagai 2.8).*"

Why then did R' Yehoshua teach that a person should engage in business honestly? – The reason is that one without the other,[24] does not work. (Nida 70b)

---

since he has prayed so well, Hashem 'owes him.' He has to pray, and then pray again, and hope with a simple hope, that Hashem's answer will be *yes*. When a person follows this formula, then our Rabbis teach, he will not return empty-handed.

[24] **One without the other** – Rebbi Yehoshua assumed originally, that the people were praying for a livelihood, and wanted to know why their prayers were not helping. He therefore told them to engage in honest business. Only later he realized their real problem; namely, that they were not praying as they should.

We *all* unfortunately, tend to disregard the power of prayer. Often, we even second it to other efforts. Contra this, our Rabbis teach, prayer is really *the most* effective and direct means we have to change our lot. Its importance overshadows any other means we have. We therefore must train ourselves to the importance of prayer.

Listen to the *Chazon Ish*: When a person acquires money and property...he should not think, G-d forbid, that *'it is his initiative and strength that makes this wealth' (Devarim 8.17).* Instead he must remember that we have no power to do anything – our deeds serve *only* to arouse the heavenly courts that we may receive that which we seek. Accordingly, one who prays with heart, and begs for his salvation, *does more* than one who makes a physical effort...

Even when the Torah requires a person to make a physical effort to save the situation, this does not exempt him from praying. Moreover, if he doesn't pray, he withholds himself from this salvation! *(Koveitz Igros 62)*

More Belief

One of the reasons Hashem wishes us to both work and pray, is that we may thereby strengthen our faith.

Not from toiling to buy and sell wares,[25] travelling from East to West, does a person become rich; even if he will sail the seas ... and encircle deserts and mountains, he will not become rich ... [unless Hashem so wishes it] (BaMidbar Raba 22.8)

The Rabbis taught: Profits made from overseas funding,[26] see no success. (Pesachim 50b)

The Evil Eye

Just as prayers help a person to success, so they may lead to his ruin. Prayers uttered by jealous people, people eager to see his downfall, release destructive forces. A spiritual power related to such "negative prayer" is the *eyn horo – the evil eye!*[27]

One who earns his income from selling twigs and earthenware pots, sees no success. Why? Since they are bulky, the evil eye rests on them.

---

[25] **Not from toiling** – A person must invest his faith only in Hashem. While Hashem fills the world with all types of opportunities, all sorts of money-making schemes, no man may lean on them. He may only view them as *tools* that Hashem gives him to channel his thoughts to his Maker. They are here to boost and strengthen his faith in Hashem.

When however, a person leans too heavily on such means, on a job, a rich father, etc., when he uses them as his crutch, he angers Hashem. Moreover, he prompts Hashem to strip him of this 'support,' or diminish it in some other way. This Hashem does for him as an act of kindness. He does not want a person to lean on cracked, crooked sticks.

[26] **From overseas funding** – When a person looks to overseas profits, he looks into the distance. However, only the Heavens are the 'far away' a person may look to. Therefore, Hashem acts kindly towards us. He withholds His blessing from such profits. In this way, He prevents us from substituting these earnings for the wealth that only the Heavens may give; He prevents us from trusting in anything besides Himself.

[27] **The evil eye** – Jealousy is a deeply felt emotion. It stabs deeply into a person's heart. It may even do so, without the jealous person feeling it. When the jealous person challenges the Heavens, asking, "why does so-and-so enjoy what I do not," he raises a heavenly storm. For the Heavens do not ignore any prayer, *especially* one that comes from the heart. Rather, they attend to his plea, and strip the other of his advantages.

Those who sell on street-corners,[28] do not succeed. Why? The evil eye rests on them.[29] (Pesachim 50b)

Discretion

A further idea is that just as a person must protect his possessions from others' eyes, so he must also protect them from *his own eye!* For only where the small human eye does not rule, may the Great Heavenly Eye bestow its blessings.

Rav Yitzchak said: Blessing is only found in that which is hidden from the eye.[30] (Baba Metzia 42a)

---

[28] **Twigs and earthenware pots...selling on street corners** – Twigs and earthenware pots are bulky, and easily attract people's attention. Selling on street corners is similarly obvious to all. This arouses the envy and ill-will of others. They see him doing 'big' business, and resent his good fortune. As a result, they subconsciously send a protest to Heaven, challenging his merits. This in turn, brings to failure and loss. Therefore, a person should seek a discreet business. And if this is not possible, he should at least conduct his affairs in a quiet, modest way.

Likewise, a person must take care not to flaunt his successes. He must not brag of his wealth, even to those who 'don't envy him.' For they too, may resent his successes, and injure him with the force of *the evil eye*.

[29] **The evil eye rests on them** – One form of business that the Rabbis recommend is breeding small livestock. They require little more than grass, and are quick to grow large and fat. Thus they are most profitable.

Rebbi Yochanan said: One who wishes to become wealthy, should raise small livestock. (Chulin 84b)

Another teaching however, contradicts this...

Those who deal in small livestock, see no success in their business. Why? – For they upset other people. (Pesachim 50b)

Rashi explains that while small farm-animals grow quickly, they are also a nuisance and damage other peoples' fields. This creates only anger and resentment. To prevent such damage and theft, the Rabbis even decreed that one may not grow small livestock in *Eretz Yisrael (Baba Kama 79b)*

Tosephos however, explains that when one lives in a town, an *evil eye* rests on his business, and this spoils his success.

How then could Rebbi Yochanan recommend such a business? – To this *Tosephos* answers that Rebbi Yochanan speaks of breeding livestock in woody areas. Here, there is little chance that they will do damage to other people's property or that the *evil eye* will rest upon them.

[30] **Hidden from the eye** – Can this be? Can a person hurt himself with his *own* eye? – The answer is yes! A person focuses on one world at a time. *Moreover*, the world

The Rabbis taught: One who goes to measure his harvest, should pray, 'May it be Your will Hashem, that You bless the work of our hands.'

But if he measures it, and then prays, he prays in vain, for Hashem does not bless that which is weighed, measured or counted; He only blesses that which is hidden from the eye. (ibid.)

Heavenly Protection

A person does not need Hashem's blessing only to enrich him. He also needs it to preserve his wealth. This too, Hashem provides.

"He will bless you, *and protect you*." (BaMidbar 6.24) How so?

A flesh and blood king who dwelt in Rome, had a servant in Suria. The king summoned him. When the servant came, he gave him a hundred measures of gold. However, as the servant went along his way, bandits fell on him and robbed him of the entire gift.

---

he looks at, is the world he lives in. Thus, when his thoughts point Heavenward, he lives in a world *'where Hashem rules all, and all is in His hands.'* When however, he trains his thoughts on this world – his own world, he must then follow the rules of nature.

When a person lives in Hashem's world, he receives Hashem's blessing. How so? – Before a person measures his harvest, he is uncertain of its yield. Thus, he may turn his gaze to the Heavens, and ask, in all sincerity, that the Heavens bless his crops. However, *after* he measures them, he now lives in his own world, and he forfeits this blessing. Since *he himself* does not believe that the size of his stores can swell, he cannot pray that Hashem increases their abundance. He lives now in a world where that which is counted, is counted, and there is no room for further growth.

This is true of all situations. As long as a person lives with an element of uncertainty, he may dream great dreams; he may throw his faith on Hashem; he may pray for astounding wealth. However, once he delineates and defines his world, he loses this power of prayer. He strips his mind of the thought that Hashem performs marvelous miracles, and thereby, restrains Hashem from enriching him.

This is one reason why Hashem hides the future from us. He wants us to strive for amazing feats, without any limits to hamper our progress!

Another way a person damages himself with his own eye, is through the attribute of arrogance. One who surveys his property, is tempted to feel that he is the master of his possessions. He considers himself somehow, as being a lord of his destiny and controlling his own world. However, no man is a master of anything in this world. Only Hashem claims this title. Such arrogance therefore, 'angers' Hashem and incites Him to strip him of his riches, or worse still, *his riches from him!*

Are we able to protect ourselves better than that poor servant? Therefore Hashem not only blesses his servants with wealth, He also protects them from bandits.[31]

Also...

He will bless you – with wealth, *and protect you* – from taxes and tax-collectors.[32]

He will bless you – with wealth, *and protect you* – that you use your riches for *mitzvos*.[33]

He will bless you – with wealth, *and protect you* – that others do not overpower you.

He will bless you – with wealth, *and protect you* – from the harmful energies and forces that surround you.[34]

He will bless you – with wealth, *and protect you* – that you do not forfeit the pact Hashem made with your fore-fathers.

He will bless you – with wealth, *and protect you* – that you do not forfeit the glorious end of days.[35]

He will bless you – with wealth, *and protect you* – that your soul is not harmed at the time of death.

He will bless you – with wealth, *and protect you* – that you are not lead to *Gehinom*.

And, in a different vein ...

He will bless you – with sons, *and protect you* – He will grace you with daughters and guard them from harm. (BaMidbar Raba 11.5)

---

[31] **He also protects them** – Hashem besides giving a person wealth, health, etc., also helps him to preserve it.

[32] **From taxes** – Hashem's does not limit His protection to keeping away bandits. There are other troubles, from which He saves a person. One such worry is unfair taxation. Another is the taxing experience and expense of falling into the hands of doctors and lawyers!

[33] **You use your riches for *mitzvos*** – Not only should wealth not stop a person from doing mitzvos, it should even help him do *more mitzvos*.

[34] **Harmful energies and forces** – Those who are rich are more vulnerable to negative spiritual forces that contaminate their minds and hearts.

[35] **The glorious end of days** – That he will not consume his eternal reward in this world.

Remember Hashem

If to ensure his success, a person must honor his friend, how much the more then, must he take care to honor Hashem.

> *David haMelech* says: "Fortunate is the man who *regards Hashem with awe, and hungers for His mitzvos*; his children will be mighty; he will be blessed with good offspring; in his house will be great wealth, and his righteousness will endure forever ... " (Tehillim 112.1-3)

For this reason, profit-making schemes that oppose Hashem's commands cannot succeed.

> Rav Huna taught: One who disregards *netilas yadaim*[36] comes to poverty. (Shabbos 62b)

> "Disregarding *netilas yadaim*," said Rava, "means that he does not wash at all, but if he does fulfill the minimum requirements, there is no problem."

> "This is not so,"[37] argues the *Gemara*, "for Rav Chisda taught: I wash with full hands of water, and receive full hands of blessing." (ibid.)

---

[36] **Netilas yadaim** – The ritual hand-washing that our Rabbis enacted whenever we waken from our sleep, pray, or eat bread or wet fruit. Disregarding even such a ruling brings a person to poverty.

A further idea, one that specifically links *netilas yadaim* with wealth, is this: In earlier times, before a *Kohen* could serve in the Temple or eat sacrificial foods, he would wash his hands. Like the *Kohen*, we too wash our hands before we pray to Hashem or partake of His food. Thus, we separate ourselves from our everyday lives, we 'wash our hands' of the mundane, and sanctify ourselves. Then, once we 'let go of this world,' we may engage in the spiritual act; then, we may enter a realm of holiness.

However, a person who is reluctant to forfeit this world's pleasures, will not create this separation. His inability to overcome his laziness or forgo his comforts, causes him to *mix* the profane with the holy. Thus, he tarnishes Heaven's glory, defiles that which is lofty and loses the ability to turn his eyes upwards. He disconnects himself from the Heavens, and the Heavens in turn, disconnect themselves from him. They withhold their blessings, and condemn him to poverty.

[37] **This is not so** – Rava learns that keeping the minimum standards, protects a person from poverty. Rav Chisda however, disputes this view.

Seemingly Rava and Rav Chisda do not argue. Rava states that if a person keeps the minimum standard, he avoids poverty; Rav Chisda says that if he *only* keeps the minimum standard, he does not receive handfuls of abundance. Why then does the *Gemara* present their views as a dispute?

In Vain

Another *mitzva* our Rabbis link to wealth and poverty is respecting Hashem's holy name.

Rav said: Where Hashem's name is mentioned[38] [in vain], there poverty is found ... (Nedarim 7b)

Lies

An extension of not mentioning Hashem's name in vain, is the duty to avoid all forms of deceit and falsehood. These too carry a heavy penalty.

He who punished the people of the *Flood* and the *tower of Bavel*, the people of *Sedom and Amora*, and Egypt at the sea – will ultimately punish all who do not keep their word. (Baba Metzia 48a)

The wealth of those who promise charity publicly[39] and don't give it, is confiscated. (Sukka 29a)

We must explain therefore, that when a person does not merit Heaven's blessings, when he does not receive these 'handfuls of abundance,' he loses something that is really his. Heaven has already given him these riches. However, in his slothfulness he drops this; with his laziness, he rejects Heaven's gift.

[38] **Where Hashem's name is mentioned** – Praising Hashem's name is a *mitzva;* for instance, when a person prays or recites a *brocha*. Such a mention brings blessing and wealth. However, when he says Hashem's name in vain, this brings to poverty. *(Ran)*

The Torah wants each person to recognize Hashem as the ultimate Master. For only by recognizing Hashem, may he build a relationship with Him. The person who utters Hashem's name with respect, already shows such an appreciation. With his reverence he synthesizes the upper, spiritual spheres with his material existence. He injects Divine values – qualities such as kindness, humility and love – into his life. This enriches his world, and fills it with blessing.

However, when he throws Hashem's name around, when he swears by it casually, he perverts this heavenly purpose. He disconnects himself from Hashem, and thereby alienates his world from its *Source of Sustenance*.

[39] **Those who promise charity** – One who breaks his word, shows his disregard for Hashem's heavenly presence. For how may he lie, while Hashem watches him? This is especially true when he breaks a pledge he made to charity or other spiritual matters. Such a disregard for Hashem, profanes His name, and brings on heavenly retribution.

Not for all the money

While we see how the Torah advises a person how to achieve greater prosperity, still it expects him to place his religious observance first. Only then may he ultimately profit.

> We do not transgress to avoid a monetary loss.[40] (Baba Metzia 30a)

A Path of Gold

When, however, we are careful to follow Hashem's commands, Hashem in His great generosity, awards us a wage. The principle of this reward He stores away for us in the world-to-come, while *the interest* this principle earns – the 'fruit' of our 'trees' – He gives us in this world. The more we realize that such interest comes from Hashem Himself, the more we appreciate and enjoy it.

> The *mitzvos* of Hashem are straight, they bring joy to the heart ... they are more desirable than gold, the finest of gold; they are sweeter than honey[41] and the drippings of honeycombs. (Tehillim 19.9,11)

> Rav Avin haLevi b'Rebbi taught: *Yisrael* became rich from the plague of blood.[42] How so?

---

[40] **We do not transgress** – A person should be ready to forfeit his *entire wealth* before he transgresses any negative command. If for example, his house is burning on Shabbos, as long as no life is in danger, he may not put it out. [There are ways however, of soliciting non-Jewish help in such situations – see *Orach Chayim 334.26 and Mishna Breura there*] With positive commands however, the Torah does not require a person to sacrifice more than a third of his wealth to fulfill a *mitzva*. (*Orach Chayim 656, Remah and Mishna Breura there*)

[41] **Sweeter than honey** – The sweetness of honey is temporary. The sweetness of *mitzvos* is eternal. Since honey is a part of our physical, limited world, its pleasures are likewise limited. Thus, for instance, too much honey makes a person sick. However, the sweetness of *mitzvos* is a part of eternity. As such, it delights and inspires a person forever.

[42]. **From the plague of blood** – Where Hashem is, there wealth is. In the plague of blood, Hashem displayed His might to the world. *Yisrael*, as Hashem's partners, was a part of this display. Their water did not become blood. Thus, they 'assisted' Hashem to perform this miracle – they were His partners. And as partners, they also made a neat profit in the process.

Similarly, they profited when they left Egypt; each one received gold and silver vessels, as well as expensive clothing. Likewise, when Hashem created the grand miracle of splitting the sea, they received yet another rich booty. Each time Hashem acted, *Yisrael* became wealthier.

If there was a barrel of water, and the Egyptian filled his jug from it, he received a jug of blood, while the *Yisrael* drank water from the barrel.

"Give me the water in your hand," the Egyptian would command. Still that which he gave him, turned to blood. Even when both drank from the same bowl, the *Yisrael* would drink water while the Egyptian drank blood.

Only when the Egyptian paid the *Yisrael* for the water, did he receive water. In this way *Yisrael* became rich. (Shmos Raba 9.10)

Yisrael took two wealths, one when they left Egypt, the other when they entered *Eretz Yisrael*.[43] (Zohar, VaYikra 50)

Here then is another way to wealth – to align oneself with Hashem's divine will. And while Hashem does not perform miracles every day, still, *"There is might and great rejoicing in His place." (Divrei haYamim 1.16)* One who lives in Hashem's palace, enjoys the benefits of this privilege.

[43] **When they entered *Eretz Yisrael*** – Hashem enriched *Yisrael* with the wealth of the nations He expelled from *Eretz Yisrael*. *Yisrael* received their homes, orchards, fields and vineyards, as well as all their gold and silver. This, together with the booty they merited on leaving Egypt, was not a wealth they worked for, but rather a gift from Hashem.

At a deeper level, the wealth they gained when they left Egypt parallels the reward a Jew receives when he obeys Hashem's command, *"Move away from evil" (Tehillim 34.15)* – while the bounty they amassed when they entered *Eretz Yisrael*, parallels their reward for fulfilling the command, *"...and do good" (ibid.)*

CHAPTER THIRTEEN

WORKING FOR HASHEM

Another Route

If a person's livelihood comes from Hashem, why must man labor? The Torah tells us that this was 'a fine' imposed on Adam when he sinned. If he doesn't work, he doesn't eat. Still there is no guarantee that the working man will succeed. His success, or lack of success, remains squarely, in Hashem's hands.

Accordingly, a person should prosper just as well, or even better, when he works for Hashem alone.

There is however, one requirement. This is that a person must realize that Hashem can and will take care of him. But, if he will not believe that Hashem supports him as he serves Hashem, then Hashem will not support him! In such a case, he will have to find a 'regular' job.

King David said: "Throw your all on Hashem,[1] and He will sustain you; He will never allow the *tzaddik* to falter." (Tehillim 65.23)

R' Nehorai said: "I disregard all the occupations in the world, and teach my son only Torah. For all occupations only stand by a person in his youth, but leave him to die of hunger in his old age. Torah however, is different; it stands by the person in his youth, and gives him a future and assurance in his old age.

In his youth the Torah promises, "Those who hope to Hashem will renew their strength, they will grow wings of eagles." (Yeshayahu 40.31)

In his old age it assures him, "The white-haired will yet blossom, they will feel strong and refreshed." (Tehillim 92.15) (Kidushin 82b)

R' Elazar said: Every man was born to labor, as the verse teaches, "A man was born to labor." (Iyov 5.7)

Still, says the gemora, we do not know what this 'labor' refers to? Is it the labor of speaking, or the labor of working?

---

[1] **Throw your all** – Stop dreaming, scheming and planning how to acquire riches. Rather, invest your ingenuity and energies into serving Hashem, and trust in Hashem to take care of your livelihood.

We are therefore, taught[2] that man was born for the labor of speaking.

Yet, still we don't know if this labor refers to speaking in Torah, or other speech?[3]

We are therefore, taught that a person was born to labor in Torah. (Sanhedrin 99b)

R' Nechunya ben HaKanna said: One who accepts the yoke of Torah, frees himself from the yoke of the working world, and the yoke of the government.[4] (Avos 3.6)

R' Shimon ben Elazar said: I never saw a deer working as a farmer, nor a lion as a porter, nor a fox as a store-keeper, yet they all receive their living without pain. Now, if they were created to serve *me* [and in this merit they receive their daily bread] surely I, who was created to serve my Creator, should receive my livelihood painlessly![5] Rather, it is through my sinful behavior that I cut short my livelihood. (Kidushin 82b)

---

[2] **We are therefore taught** – The Torah educates us as to the nature and purpose of man's stay in this world. By way of its verses we learn:

(a) that man was originally created to labor with his mouth and not his body – thus, the verse that states: "His mouth labors" (Mishle 16.26); and

(b) that the type of labor he should use his mouth for, is **learning and teaching Torah** – as the verse states: "This Torah shall not depart from your mouth." (Yehoshua 1.8)

[3] **Other speech** – How could we imagine that a person fulfills his duty to labor with 'other speech'? The answer is that when he counsels, advises or teaches people the ways of the world, he serves a life-giving function. Man is a social being, and one who helps him live in society, advances his welfare and thereby, fulfills one of his duties to Hashem. Thus, the Gemara considers this as a possible reason why man was born.

[4] **The yoke of the government** – This is the payment of taxes or serving the country in a physical sense, e.g., in the army.

[5] **I should receive my livelihood painlessly** – When a person fulfills the purpose for which Hashem created him, Hashem will not hold back any part of his livelihood. It is only when he squanders his time, when he chases fantasies instead of Torah and mitzvos, that he angers Hashem. "Since you will not labor on My behalf," Hashem tells him, "I will force you to labor on your own behalf. If you wish to eat, go and work!"

In such a case, forcing a man to work, is an act of kindness from Hashem. For he only lives healthily, happily, when he is busy. This the Torah states explicitly: "A man was born to labor" (Iyov 5). Furthermore, when he does not work, he comes to sin. (See Avos 2.2) Therefore, to prevent this, the Heavens force him to toil.

In vain, you arise early and stay up late, to eat the bread of your toil;[6] those who are beloved [to Hashem, receive the same sustenance – even when] they sleep well. (Tehillim 127.2, Malbim there)

When a person wishes to labor in Torah, Heaven permits him to do so. When a person wishes to labor in this world, this too, Heaven permits him.[7] (Tana d'Bei Eliyahu Raba 13)

Opposing Views

R' Yishmael asked, the verse states: "You shall gather in your grain..." (Devarim 11.14) Isn't this obvious? What is the point of this teaching?!

Rather, he taught, since there is a verse that reads, "This book of Torah shall never leave your mouth," (Yehoshua 1.8) I might think that this is literal, i.e., that one must never cease studying. Therefore this verse comes to tell us that we must also conform with the ways of the world[8] – if we wish to eat, we must work.

R' Shimon ben Yochai however, argues with this view: If a man plows in the plowing season, sows in the sowing season, harvests in the harvest-time, threshes in the threshing season, winnows in the windy season, what will be of the Torah?!

Rather, the verse, "You shall gather in your grain" teaches the following: When Yisrael does Hashem's will, their work is done for them by others,[9]

---

[6] **In vain, you arise early and stay up late** – One who toils continuously, does so in vain. Hashem has set his livelihood, and all his efforts will not increase it. By working longer hours, he is like the man who fits a second tap to his wine barrel. While at first, he receives more wine, his supply soon runs out. (Chafetz Chaim)

[7] **Heaven permits him** – There are two paths in life: One is to work for Hashem; the other is to work for oneself. What people fail to realize though, is that when the person works for Hashem, he also works for himself; for as he concerns himself with Hashem's desires, so Hashem concerns Himself with his desires. In a similar vein our Rabbis teach:

Do His will as though it were your own, that He may do your will, as though it were His own. (Avos 2.4)

[8] **We must also conform with the ways of the world** – Rebbi Yishmael proposes a path that combines yeshiva studies with working.

[9] **Their work is done for them by others** – Rebbi Shimon defines the Torah path thus: For a Yisrael to fulfill his role in the world, he must dedicate himself to Torah study. Hashem in turn, will send him his livelihood in wondrous ways, and he need not work at all. Should he, however, not sacrifice himself for his Torah study, he sins. And the punishment for this sin is that he must go out to work!

but when they don't do His will, then they must work themselves, as the verse says "You shall gather in your grain." (Brochos 35b)

On this Abaye commented: Those who did like R' Yishmael succeeded,[10] while those who did like R' Shimon ben Yochai, did not succeed. (ibid.)

Similarly, Rava said to his students, "I beg you do not come to me in Tishrei and Nisan[11] – the harvest and sowing seasons – so that your livelihood should not preoccupy you all year round!" (ibid.)

Top Priority

While the general view is that even a Torah scholar should combine his Torah studies with work,[12] still he should keep this work to the necessary minimum; as Shammai the Elder said: "Give priority to your Torah studies."[13] (Avos 1.14) Make sure your Torah learning is firm and solid – that it is the most important of all your occupations – while your work in contrast, remains a secondary and incidental interest.

Rabba bar bar Chana, in the name of R' Yochanan, in the name of R' Ilai, said: Come and see how the later generations do not match the early

---

[10] **Many did like R' Yishmael and succeeded** – The path R' Yishmael proposes is an approach that best fits the belief level and spiritual temperament of most people. Thus, when they follow this path, they succeed. On the other hand, when these same people follow R' Shimon's path, they fail. Since they lack the vision to plunge into a full Torah life, they forfeit this special heavenly help – they do not merit that others do their work for them.

Still, a person who aspires to great heights, who has grand goals and lofty ambitions, should follow the more idealistic path. If he believes that he can do it, the Heavens will help him realize his dream. They will plot for him a path that leads to every success and prosperity.

[11] **Do not come to me in Tishrei and Nisan** – Rava also instructed his students to follow R' Yishmael's teaching. Still, we see here that he understands R' Yishmael's way as meaning that the student should toil no more than two months a year! The rest of the year he should devote solely to his Torah studies.

[12] **Torah studies with work** – However, if the community supports Torah scholars, it is better that he studies Torah full-time, and relies on others to sustain his household. This is especially true for our times, where the generation's faith is so weak. Now, more than ever, there is a great and holy duty for anyone who can, to devote his strengths to Torah study, and allow the community to support him. (Chafetz Chaim, Shem Olam, ch.11)

[13] **Give priority to your Torah studies** – Even when a person spends most of his day working, still he must give his Torah lessons top priority. The time he spends learning should be the highlight of his day, his first interest and love.

generations. The early generations made their Torah studies their main occupation, and their livelihood incidental – and they succeeded at both. However the later generations make their livelihood their main occupation, and their Torah studies incidental, and do not succeed at either.[14] (Brochos 35b)

The Torah Way

To succeed in ones Torah studies, a person must pour great enthusiasm and energy into it. He must give it the love and devotion that a good businessman gives to his business. Then he may enjoy the happiness and triumph that comes from following this path.

David haMelech says: I rejoice in Your teachings [Hashem], as I would rejoice over all wealth. (Tehillim 119.14)

Better is the Torah of Your mouth [Hashem], than thousands of gold and silver. (ibid.72)

I love Your mitzvos more than gold. (ibid.127)

Rava said: All bodies were born to labor;[15] happy is he who labors in Torah. (Sanhedrin 99b)

R' Yochanan, on completing the book of Iyov would say: Man's end is death,[16] and a beast's end is slaughter; all must eventually die. Happy

---

[14] **They do not succeed at either** – There are two paths in life, and not three. One may devote himself to Hashem and enjoy the protection Hashem gives to those who serve Him; or he may leap into the pleasures of this world, following the philosophy of "Eat, drink and be merry, for tomorrow we die." (Yeshayahu 22.13) However, if he tries to grasp both ways, if he dances at two weddings, he will fail at them both.

The best advice then, for the person who wants to enjoy this world, as well as the world-to-come, is to throw himself fully into serving Hashem. In this way, he builds up his next world, while Hashem satisfies his needs in this one. This approach accords with the teaching: He who wants to live, should kill himself. (Tamid 32a)

[15] **All bodies were born to labor** – Every person must labor. Even if he avoids working, he will suffer other forms of grief and anxiety . These too, are forms of labor. Thus, we see that the Hebrew word 'amal' (עָמָל), means both labor and suffering.

[16] **Man's end is death** – If a person could live in this world forever, there would be good reason to invest great energies into building palaces of pleasure and comfort. However, since he only passes through this world, he is better off not getting too comfortable here. This only makes it the harder for him, when he has to leave.

therefore, is one who lives on Torah, who labors in Torah, and who pleases his Maker. (Brochos 17a)

Reish Lakish dedicated himself fully to his Torah studies. He would work only to earn that day's allowance. "Why should I set food aside for tomorrow, when I could be learning?" he would say, "Who says I will even be alive then!"

Thus, when he died, all he left behind was a little saffron. Still, he bemoaned even this. "Of one like me the verse says," he told his students, "'they leave their wealth to others'. (Tehillim 49.11)" (Gitin 47a)

Elazar haKappar taught, "Let a person pray always to be saved from poverty – even if he can avoid poverty, it may come upon his son; and if not on his son, then on his grandson...as the Yeshiva of R' Yishmael taught, "There is a wheel of fortune that revolves in the world."

Rav Yosef said, "A dedicated Torah scholar however, does not become poor."

"But we see poor scholars?" his students objected.

While they may be poor," he answered, "they need not beg from door to door."[17] (Shabbos 151b)

Torah Rewards

Counsel and salvation are mine, [declares the Torah,] I am understanding, victory is mine; kings rule with me ... ministers reign with me ... wealth and honor are by me, rare treasuries and great charities; my fruit is better than gold – than the finest gold, and my produce is choice silver ... those that love me, inherit wealth;[18] I will fill their store rooms. (Mishle 8.14-21)

The words of Torah are poor in one place, and rich in another.[19] (Yerushalmi Rosh HaShana 3.5)

---

[17] **They need not beg** – Even the poorest of students, the one least devoted and dedicated to his studies, need not feel the shame of begging for food.

[18] **Those that love me, inherit wealth** – In their love of the Torah, they pursue its every hint and nuance; their learning is rich and full. In turn, the Torah enriches and fills every aspect of their life.

[19] **Poor in one place, and rich in another** – Torah itself, is a type of wealth. The words of Torah in one place may be rich; they may be rich in content and original thoughts. In another place however, they may be poor; they may be scant in number and remote of any understanding. Our duty is to ensure that all the Torah's words are rich. Therefore, we must delve into their depths and discover

R' Chama b'Rebbi Chanina taught: Moshe became wealthy from the chippings of the tablets.[20] (Nedarim 38a)

"The blessing of Hashem enriches, without adding pain." (Mishle 10.22)

R' Tanchuma taught that this verse hints to Moshe. Hashem told Moshe carve out two tablets, showing him a block of sapphire stone in his tent, from which he could carve them out. "The leftover carvings are for you," Hashem told him, and from this Moshe became a king.[21]

From here you learn that all who occupies himself with Torah, receives his livelihood from the Torah; moreover, he becomes rich and successful. And what does the rest of the verse "...*without adding pain*," refer to? – This shows that Hashem did not trouble Moshe to travel afar; rather He prepared for Moshe all that he needed, in his own tent! (Tanchuma Tisa 29)

There are "length of days,[22] at the Torah's right;[23] [while] at its left, are riches and honor." (Mishle 3.16)

---

their pearls; we must remove the dust of misunderstanding, and polish the existing reasonings; until their knowledge shines like fine gold. Then we too may benefit from their wealth. (Based on a thought of Rav Pesach Rosenzweig)

[20] **The chippings of the tablets** – Even the 'waste product' of the Torah, the stone that was discarded to make way for the Torah's letters, has a very great value.

[21] **From this Moshe became a king** – There is no activity in this world that does not contain some waste. This idea of waste has important kabbalistic ramifications. Simply speaking though, it is the separation of evil from good, of unholy from holy. Moshe's acts however, were on such a high level, that his waste was pure sapphire.

How, we may ask, did he merit this? – Moshe, as leader of the Jewish people, never sought wealth for himself. He never used his position to enhance his personal fortunes. On the contrary, he so occupied himself with the people's needs, that he gave nothing to his self. The Torah even relates that as he descended Mount Sinai, he went straight to the people. He did not stop at his home, even for a moment. (Rashi, Shmos 19.14).

The Torah however, demands that every effort receives its compensation, even in this world. Thus, Moshe, in proportion with his exalted position, had to receive an exalted wealth. Still, since he would not take from others, his reward had to come in a roundabout way. This was through the chippings, the waste product of his own labors. It was these carvings that endowed him with a fabulous fortune.

Similarly, all who toil over the Torah, or serve Hashem in some way, receive a handsome reward. Hashem pays them in full for their every labor, effort, inconvenience and concern.

[22] **Length of days** – This refers to the world-to-come.

"Does this mean," asked Rav Sheishes, "that those who cling to *"its right"* receive length of days, but no wealth and honor?

"Rather," he replied, "it means that those who cling to its right, receive length of days, and all the more so, wealth and honor;[24] but those at its left receive only wealth and honor, but not length of days. (Shabbos 63a)

---

[23] **At the Torah's right** – This refers to the scholars who labor in the Torah with skill and determination, like one who works with his right hand; while **at its left** refers to those who learn Torah in a slack way, like one who does something with his weaker hand.

Also, **at the Torah's right** indicates those who learn with pure motivations, i.e., for the sake of the Torah itself, while **at its left** points to those who learn with impure and wicked motivations. (Rashi)

[24] **Length of days, and all the more so, wealth and honor** – There are three types of Torah scholars. One is the scholar who reads through the Torah, enjoying the ideas and insights he picks up along the way. The second is the scholar who makes the effort to acquire and possess the Torah he learns; he reviews it many times, until he knows it by heart. The third however, is the greatest of all. He delves to the depths of studies, investing in it concentration and great energy, until he understands the law at its roots. The second scholar is the one 'who learns Torah with his left hand.' The third is the one 'who learns Torah with his right.'

Hashem rewards the three types generously, but differently. The first scholar receives the reward for learning Torah. Since each word of Torah he recites is a mitzva, and since each of these mitzvos carries the weight of all 613 mitzvos (Yerushalmi, Peah ch.1), he receives a reward of tremendous value.

The second scholar, besides the reward of the first, receives wealth and honor in this world. Hashem created this world with the Torah, and so the scholar who possesses this Torah, gains access to its power over this world; he wins its treasures and pleasures, its riches and glories. Still, since he learnt the Torah superficially – with his left hand – he possesses only the external aspect of the Torah, its body but not its soul. Thus, he does not enjoy the special reward that belongs to the third scholar...

The third scholar acquires the most wondrous prize of all. Since he grasps the deeper, inner quality, or 'soul' of the Torah, he gains entrance – title and mastery – to the highest level of the world-to-come. This distinction is unique to him.

Rav Sheishes however, adds here an amazing idea. This is that even though the third scholar does not actively memorize his studies, still he receives all that the second scholar achieves. This is mastery over the body of the Torah, together with the wealth and honor this mastery gives him. For once he understands the Torah to its depths, he possesses it in the fullest sense possible.

R' Yonasan said: All who toil over the Torah in poverty, ultimately toil over it in wealth. Conversely, all who are lazy to study Torah, despite their wealth, are ultimately lazy to study it, in poverty.[25] (Avos 4.9)

With Honor

R' Yosi says: One who honors the Torah, receives honor.[26] (Avos 4.6)

Rebbi asked R' Yishmael b'Rebbi Yosi, "How do the wealthy of *Eretz Yisrael* merit their wealth?"

"Through tithing their income," he answered.

"And how do the wealthy in *Bavel* merit their wealth?" he asked.

"Through honoring the Torah."[27] (Shabbos 119a)

One who walks to the Beis haMedresh, even if he doesn't learn, receives reward.[28] (Avos 5.14)

Hashem does not crush the reward of any creature.[29] (Pesachim 118a)

---

[25] **Lazy to study it, in poverty** – The scholar who invests his main strengths into learning Torah, has the correct priorities. Therefore, he may enjoy Heaven's blessings. However, if this prosperity distracts him from his studies, he forfeits them. Heaven prefers him to lose his petty riches, that he might gain instead the most precious treasure of all, the holy Torah.

[26] **Receives honor** – A person may think that the wealth and honor that come with Torah studies, are only for its most outstanding scholars. We learn here that this is not so. Even one who is not a scholar, yet he honors the Torah, receives such blessings.

[27] **Through honoring the Torah** – The function of tithes is to enhance the service of Hashem. For these tithes sustain the Kohanim and Leviim, that they may give their all to promote and glorify Torah study and practice. Thus, the person who gives tithes, promotes their holy service. This entitles him in turn, to great heavenly blessings.

In Bavel, where the laws of tithes do not apply, a person gains this merit by supporting Torah scholars. When he provides these scholars with a living, together with the recognition and respect they so deserve, he likewise enhances and sanctifies Hashem's name. This earns him Heaven's gratitude and blessings.

[28] **Even if he doesn't learn** – but only listens to others. (Rashi)

[29] **Any creature** – No matter what a person does, if he does it for Hashem, or at least, because Hashem commands it, he receives reward.

Torah Support

One who marries his daughter to a Torah scholar, does business with a Torah scholar, and enriches a Torah scholar, is considered as though he clings to the Divine Presence.[30] (Kesuvos 111b)

R' Tarfon once gave R' Akiva six hundred *zuz*. "Go, buy a field," he told him, "that you and I may learn Torah, while it sustains us."

R' Akiva took the money, and distributed it amongst Torah students.

A few days later R' Tarfon was speaking with R' Akiva, and asked him whether he had bought the field.

"Yes," R' Akiva told him.

"May I see it," R' Tarfon asked.

"Certainly," R' Akiva answered. He then took him and showed him the students engaged in their studies.

R' Tarfon however thought that R' Akiva had bought the field and then sold it to these students. "Does a man give away his property for nothing?" R' Tarfon said, "Show me our profits?"

"They are with David, King of Yisrael," answered R' Akiva, "for he taught us: He who scatters his wealth amongst the poor, establishes his righteousness forever.[31]" (Tehillim 112) (VaYikra Raba 34.16)

And look ...

Hashem enriched R' Akiva[32] six times.[33] (Nedarim 50a – see notes)

---

[30] **He clings to the Divine Presence** – There is nothing dearer to Hashem than Torah study. Thus, one who helps the scholars reach new heights of learning, also reaches new and great heights. Hashem draws very very close to him.

[31] **Establishes his righteousness forever** – Rebbi Akiva felt that scholars of his and Rebbi Tarfon's stature, should not engage in business. Instead, they should trust in Hashem to feed them. So rather than 'waste' this money on a farming venture, he used it to support other scholars – an investment that pays dividends, forever.

[32] **Hashem enriched R' Akiva** – Hashem enriched R' Akiva six times. His first fortune came from his father-in-law, one of the wealthiest men of his time. He gave R' Akiva half of his fortune. Why, we may then ask, did Hashem need to enrich him another five times? Was this first fortune not enough?

It would seem however, that R' Akiva supported Torah scholars most generously, and quickly spent this fortune. Likewise, he gave away the subsequent wealth he received. Still R' Akiva deserved to be a rich man; and so Hashem continued to send him riches.

[33] **Six times** – One, through Kalba Savua; when R' Akiva was still an unlearned shepherd, he married the daughter of Kalba Savua, one of the wealthiest and

influential men of his time. Kalba Savua swore that the couple would receive no benefit from his property. They married in the winter, and slept in a straw shed...

"Go learn in yeshiva," she told him. So he learned for twelve years with R' Yehoshua and R' Eliezer. At the end of twelve years he came home. As he stood behind the house, he overheard a wicked man taunting his wife: "Your father acted wisely. One, you are from an important family, while Akiva comes from nowhere. And two, he has left you a widow for all these years."

"If he would listen to me," she declared, "he would stay another twelve years."

"Now that I have permission, I will return to the yeshiva," R' Akiva said to himself. He returned for another twelve years.

When at last he returned home, twenty-four thousand students accompanied him ... Kalba Savua, on hearing that an important scholar had come to town, (and not realizing that this was his son-in-law), came to ask that he release him from his vow.

"You are released, you are released!" R' Akiva told him, and then revealed his identity. Kalba Savua subsequently gave him half his wealth.

...two, through a ship's ram: At the head of every ship they would carve a ram's head, as an omen that the ship would be as light as a ram. They would then fill it up with golden coins. Once sailors forgot such a head on the beach, and R' Akiva came by and found it.

...three, through a ship's treasure-box: Once R' Akiva gave four coins to some sailors. "Bring me something..." he told them. All they managed to find was a box on the beach. They brought this to him. "Wait," they told him, "and we will look for more."

He discovered that this box was from a ship that had drowned at sea. Into this box the travelers had placed all their gold coins and other treasures.

...four, through a wealthy woman: Once R' Akiva and his students needed a loan. They went to a certain wealthy woman to request this.

"You will be the debtor," she told them, "and Hashem and the sea, the guarantors." She fixed a date for repayment.

When this time came, she went down to the sea and cried out: "Lord of the universe, You know that R' Akiva is sick now, and does not have the money to pay back the loan; remember that You are the Guarantor!"

At that moment, Caesar's daughter lost her mind, and threw a box of jewels and gold coins into the sea; and the sea brought this money to the wealthy woman.

A short while later R' Akiva recovered and came to repay his loan. "Your Guarantor has already repaid the whole loan; moreover I am giving you the surplus wealth He sent me." From this money, R' Akiva became wealthy.

...five, through Turnos Rupus's wife: Rupus was one of Caesar's ministers. He was obsessed with embarrassing R' Akiva before the Caesar. However, each time R' Akiva would answer him wisely, and humiliate him. Once Rupus came home burning with anger.

"What's wrong?" his wife asked him.

Torah Power

Those who invest their energies and thoughts into Torah study, are infused with the Torah's power. This is especially so with our great Torah leaders. We must learn then to appreciate them properly.

"It's that R' Akiva ... every day he overturns me with his words," he replied.

"His G-d hates obscenity," she told her husband, "give me your permission, and I will trip him up with sin." He granted her permission. His wife, an exceptionally beautiful woman, adorned herself and set out to seduce R' Akiva.

When R' Akiva saw her, he spat, laughed and cried.

"Why these three strange reactions?" she asked him.

"Two I will explain, the third I will not," he answered; "I spat when I saw that you came from a putrid drop, and I cried that your beauty will eventually rot in the grave."

She begged him to also reveal why he had laughed.

Finally he told her, "I see that you will eventually convert to Judaism, and that I will marry you." (R' Akiva was a widower at this time.)

"What, is it still possible to repent?!" she asked incredulously.

"Yes," he answered her.

She left her husband, converted and married him, bringing into their marriage a great fortune.

...and six, from Kita bar Shalom: There was a Caesar who bitterly hated the Jews.

"One who has a dead limb," he asked his dignitaries, "should he amputate it, thereby healing himself, or leave it and suffer? (He referred here to the Jewish people, who were to his sorrow, a part of Roman Empire.)

"Amputate!" they declared.

"You can't do it," responded Kita bar Shalom, a wealthy (non-Jewish) Roman, "first, Yisrael is as indispensable to the world as the four winds (for only as long as there is a people who fulfill Hashem's Torah, will Hashem maintain this world); and second, people will call you a 'Crippled Empire.'"

"You have answered well," said Caesar, "but one who bests the king, is thrown into a house of sand (where he dies a painful death)."

As they took him to his death, one woman called out, "Woe to the ship that sails without paying its taxes!" (Kita had bravely defended the Jewish people and sanctified Hashem's name, but now was to die, without circumcising himself and converting to Judaism.)

On hearing this, he fell on his fore-skin, and cut it off.

"I have paid my tax; let me sail on." he called, "Also, I want all my wealth to go to R' Akiva."

At this a heavenly voice called out: We invite Kita bar Shalom to life in the world-to-come. (Nedarim 50a, Kesuvos 62b, Avoda Zara 10b, and adjoining commentaries)

Thus, says Hashem to Yisrael: I sent you three envoys, Moshe, Aaron and Miriam. Did they ever take your food? Did they take your drink? Did they trouble you to serve them?

On the contrary, their merit sustains you!

- In Moshe's merit, you ate mann.
- In Miriam's merit, you drank from the well.
- In Aaron's merit, clouds of glory sheltered you. (VaYikra Raba 27.6)

Rav Huna said: The speech of the Rabbis[34] brings blessing, the speech of the Rabbis enriches, the speech of the Rabbis heals. (Kesuvos 103a)

On the other hand ...

Raban Shimon ben Gamliel said: Wherever the Rabbis cast their eyes, they cause either death or poverty.[35] (Moed Katan 17b)

Special Living

Hashem expressly sanctified the Kohanim and Leviim to serve Him. For this reason Hashem gave them no part of Eretz Yisrael. He wanted them to be totally free to serve Him. When they meet this ideal, they merit special blessings.

The Rambam writes that while Hashem designated an elite group to live this elevated life-style, any person may choose to live like this; any person

---

[34] **The speech of the Rabbis** – The Rabbis know the will of Hashem. They know how to please Him. With their thoughts they enter His innermost sanctuaries; they observe His most delicate operations. They understand how the world runs, that which is fixed and that which may yet change; and where change is possible, they know how to effect this.

One who obeys the speech of the Rabbis, benefits greatly. Just listening to them, gives him merit. How much more this is so, when he follows their words. Through this he fulfills Hashem's wishes, in the best possible way, and in return, receives Hashem's blessing. He no longer withholds Hashem from enriching him; he no longer prevents Hashem from healing his wounds.

[35] **Death or poverty** – While a person should not hurt any being, even an animal, he must be especially careful not to hurt or anger a Torah scholar.

Those who insult a Torah sage, or sin in his presence, must suffer for their foolishness. For a sage connects himself closely to Hashem's innermost desires, his sighs and groans bring down great heavenly censure and punishment. How much more this is true if he is angered; as Hillel told the man who provoked him (to win a wager): "It is better that you lose four hundred zuz, and yet another four hundred zuz, rather then have Hillel lose his temper." (Shabbos 31a)

may volunteer to be a soldier in Hashem's special army, and enjoy the benefits that come with this job. (Hilchos Shmitta v'Yoveil 13.13)

One such benefit is prosperity.

Most *Kohanim* are wealthy. (Sifri Brocha 352)

No man could bring the incense offering a second time;[36] the reason is that such service makes a person wealthy. (Yoma 26a)

And of the greatest of the Kohanim the Torah teaches...

R' Yermiah taught: The Kohen Gadol should be greater than his brothers in beauty, power, wisdom and wealth.

Others say: If he does not have his own wealth, his fellow-Kohanim should enrich him from their own resources. (Horios 9a)

Since the Kohanim are Hashem's special army, one must exercise care in his dealings with them...

A Yisrael who marries a Kohen's daughter,[37] does not create a successful match. Either he widows her,[38] divorces her, or has no children. According to another teaching: She buries him before his time, or he buries her before her time, or he becomes poor.

---

[36] **A second time** – Since all the Kohanim wished to do this service, they would therefore, not allow anyone to do it twice. (Rashi) About the incense offering our Rabbis teach:

It is one of the most cherished of services (Rashi. BaMidbar 16.6).

A great column of smoke would rise from it to the Heavens, a column as straight as a stick, despite the winds that blew into it. (Avos 5.7)

Its scent filled the streets, such that no woman ever wore perfume there. (Yoma 39b)

Thus, the incense sanctified Hashem's name. Through it all realized that they were only in this world, to serve Hashem. And since it was the man who offered the incense that helped people to bless Hashem, so Hashem in turn, helped him to prosper.

Likewise, a person who fills his life with pleasant, attractive deeds, sanctifies Hashem's name. As such, he resembles the incense. He too causes others to bless Hashem, while Hashem in turn, blesses him, and sends him prosperity.

[37] **A Kohen's daughter** – Or has any other dealings, whether business or personal. In our times, this teaching applies not so much to Kohanim, but rather to those who are Torah Rabbis, and serve Hashem full-time.

[38] **He widows her** – This teaching equates: the loss of a spouse, the lack of children, death, and poverty. All of them lead to misery, as well as the loss of self-worth, security, happiness and well-being.

On this the *Gemara* asks: Surely we learnt that one who wishes to become wealthy should cling to Aaron's seed, i.e., he should marry into a family of *Kohanim*?

This teaching, answers the Gemara, speaks of the man who devotes his energies to Torah study. The first teaching however, speaks of the man who invests his energies into worldly matters.[39] (Pesachim 49a)

A Warning

Torah-study receives great dividends, dividends greater than all the mitzvos together may earn. Still, our Rabbis warn us not to learn Torah for its rewards; and especially not for its reward in this world.

R' Tarfon taught: If you have learnt much Torah, you will receive much reward ... but know that the reward of the righteous is in the world-to-come.[40] (Avos 2.16)

---

[39] **Into worldly matters** – There are two ways to succeed in this world; one, the material way, the other, along more spiritual paths.

Picture two men: Reuven has strong spiritual inclinations. He devotes his day to study and prayer. He may engage in a little business on the side, but in a minimal way. He invests his main interest into serving Hashem with all his strength. In turn, Hashem blesses his effort. He has a fine family. He lives in comfort. He enjoys an excellent reputation.

Shimon lives very much in this world. His forcefulness and ingenuity go towards building up and acquiring more material possessions. He keeps to the rules of society; he complies with religious law, but his heart is really in his business. He strives to succeed in this world, and Hashem blesses his efforts with wealth and success.

If Shimon however, turns his glance to Reuven's lot, if he decides to – marry his wealth to the holy man's prestige – his lot will turn sour. For his desire is for glory, and not spiritual elevation. Therefore such a marriage only defaces Hashem's holy name; and his efforts will end in miserable failure, and even poverty and death.

However, if he marries into Reuven's family for pure reasons, if he yearns for spirituality, for a closeness with Hashem, his marriage will succeed. His effort to marry into Reuven's family adds glory to Hashem's name, and Hashem will bless his efforts.

The Kohen in the above teaching, represents Reuven. The Yisrael represents Shimon. If the Yisrael marries into the Kohen's family with the wrong intention, he mixes water and oil, and will not succeed. However, if he himself also aspires to spiritual heights, he wins on all fronts.

[40] **The world-to-come** – The wealth the true Torah scholar receives in this world is not his reward. Heaven gives it to him as a tool, a tool that will help him to learn

Learn Torah for nothing, and not for wages; just as Hashem gave the Torah for nothing.[41] (Derech Eretz Zuta 4)

R' Tzadok said: Do not make the Torah a crown to lord over others, and do not use it as a spade to dig with[42] [and thereby earn your living]. (Avos 4.5)

Hillel said: One who takes benefit from the Torah's words, takes his own life.[43] (ibid.)

Are you serving Hashem?

No person, even when he lives in the working world, is free of serving Hashem. Whatever field of life he chooses, he must adjust his lifestyle to comply with Hashem's wishes. If he doesn't do so, he will have to answer, with much pain and shame, for his behavior.

"And you will be for Me," [says Hashem,] a kingdom of *Kohanim*.[44] (Shmos 19.6)

The poor and the wealthy ... come before Heavenly Judgment. To the poor man they say, "Why did you not learn Torah?"

If he responds that he was poor, and concerned with his livelihood, they demand: "Surely you were not as poor as Hillel?" About Hillel, the great

---

further, deeper, and with peace of mind. Therefore, when he sees that his property holdings are small, this does not upset him. He realizes that this too, is for his benefit. For it is specifically through the hardships he faces in this world, that he achieves greatness.

[41] **Hashem gave the Torah for nothing** – The greatest level a person can aim for, is to resemble Hashem. Thus, just as Hashem gives us the Torah for free – as a pure act of kindness – so we should learn it for free. We should submerge ourselves in it as a pure gift to Hashem, and not for any reward.

[42] **To dig with** – A person who uses the Torah to achieve fame and fortune, lowers and defiles it.

[43] **He takes his own life** – He eats the reward for his Torah study in this world. (Rashi)

[44] **A kingdom of** Kohanim – Every Yisrael has a potential to become a spiritual leader, a teacher. Hashem expects him to portray the Torah ideal to others, even to the world's nations. This is his responsibility to others. For if he will not teach them of Hashem's wishes through becoming a shining example, how else will they learn?

Correspondingly, when a person does serve as such an example, when he does devote himself to this ideal, Hashem helps him; Hashem assists him to make the right impression. And one of the ways He does so, is by enriching him.

Elder, they said that he would work only enough to earn a *tarpik* (a small coin). Half of this he would give to the *yeshiva's* janitor that he may enter the *yeshiva* and learn there, while the other half he used to feed his family.[45]

Similarly they ask the rich man, "Why did you not learn Torah?" If he replies that he was rich and preoccupied with his property, they respond: "Surely you were not as rich as R' Elazar ben Charsom?" About R' Elazar they said that his father left him one thousand towns on land, and correspondingly, one thousand ships at sea. Still, each day R' Elazar would take a pouch of flour on his shoulder[46] and travel from town to town, and district to district, to learn Torah.

Thus, Hillel condemns the poor, and R' Elazar ben Charsom condemns the rich. (Yoma 35b)

Hashem even enforces such a level of dedication ...

Rav Chanan said, "If the Torah promises that 'at its left are riches and honor' (Mishle 3.16), why then are my children poor?"

"They are only kept poor in this world," a heavenly voice called back to him, "so they won't preoccupy themselves with nonsense,[47] and forget the Torah." (Shocher Tov, Tehillim 5)

Rabba said: Householders who fix their Shabbos meal at the time of the Shabbos *shiurim* lose their wealth...[48]

---

[45] **To feed his family** – While Hillel understood that he must work to support his family, he also asked his family to make do with necessities alone. Thus, they helped him to study Torah most of his day.

[46] **A pouch of flour** – While Rebbi Elazar could have surrounded himself with servants and learnt Torah in great comfort, he chose to live in the simplest possible way. He knew that luxurious living would distract his thoughts from his studies, and ultimately rob him of the Torah's crown.

In a similar vein our Rabbis teach: The words of Torah are not established by the scholar who learns them lazily, and in luxury, while eating and drinking; rather by the scholar who kills himself over them. (Rambam. Hilchos Talmud Torah 3.12)

[47] **With nonsense** – However their reward in the world-to-come will be great and glorious.

[48] **At the time of the Shabbos** shiurim – When a person works to promote the Torah, either by studying and teaching it, or encouraging others to keep it, he receives a special heavenly help. Hashem knows that it is easier for a wealthy man to influence others, and so He increases this person's wealth.

On the other hand, when a person exerts a negative influence on others, he rouses Hashem to diminish and negate the effect of his actions. A wealthy man who feasts

There was a certain very wealthy household in Yerushalayim. Still, since the members of this family would fix their Shabbos meal at the time of the *Shabbos shiur*, they lost all their wealth. (Gitin 38b)

Rav Katina taught: The rains only cease because of a deficiency of Torah-learning.[49]

What is the remedy?

Increased prayer. (Taanis 7b)

R' Elazar stated: All the families of the world only receive their blessings because of *Yisrael* ...[50] Likewise, punishment only comes to the world because of *Yisrael*. (Yevamos 63a)

---

at the time of the Shabbos shiur is an example of such a person. When others see that this rich, important man doesn't attend the shiur, they too stop coming. This weakens the Torah. At this point Hashem does him a kindness; He rids him of his ability to influence others. How? – By stripping him of his wealth.

[49] **Because of a deficiency of Torah-learning** – Earlier (p.89), we quoted a teaching that it is theft that holds back the rains; while here we learn that it is lack of Torah study. Is this not a contradiction?

Our Masores however, tells us to view differing views like these, in harmony. If we probe a little, we will find a resolution. One approach is to say that each teaching addresses a different group of people.

Thus, the first teaching speaks of those who are not Torah scholars. Such people must at least, retain a high standard of integrity. If they don't do so, but instead resort to theft or other crooked activities, Hashem will punish them. He will withhold His rains, and other material blessings.

On the other hand, the second group, the Torah scholars, may not rest on their laurels. They may not smugly think that they are righteous enough. At their level, Hashem expects them to pour all their strengths into their studies. If they don't do so, Hashem will withhold His life-giving rains.

Thus, Hashem demands that each group maintain and develop the spirituality they already possess. Those who know the value of good, ethical behavior must be true to their understanding, while those who appreciate the value of Torah study, must toil diligently to further their knowledge.

[50] **Because of Yisrael** – One may live his life in one of two ways; either in the Torah world, or outside it. Likewise, he may gain his wealth in one of two ways, either the Torah way, or the non-Torah way. Still, since ultimately, the whole Creation is all for the sake of the Torah, therefore all is for the sake of Yisrael, who are the Torah's guardians.

For example: Hashem may give wealth to those nations that help Yisrael serve Hashem, while He impoverishes the nations that hinder their spiritual progress.

For His Sake Only

While living a life of mitzvos brings us to a richer life, we should not should not serve Hashem with this end in mind. Thus, our Rabbis teach: Do not be servants who serve their Master to receive a prize. (Avos 1.3)

We may serve Hashem only (1) as an expression of our gratitude for all He does for us, and (2) that we may draw closer to His awesome greatness. An interesting rule that results from this, is that the person who does mitzvos expressly that they may enrich him, does not become richer.

> The Rabbis taught: Profits made through orphans' funds do not succeed.[51]

> The Rabbis taught: Profits that come from writing or dealing in Sifrei Torah, tefillin and mezuzos; and wages earned from giving over Torah teachings...see no success.[52] (Pesachim 50b)

> The men of the great assembly sat twenty-four fasts so that scribes of Sifrei Torah, tefillin and mezuzos, should not become wealthy – for were they to become wealthy they would stop writing.[53] (ibid.)

Alternatively: Hashem may enrich those nations that (Heaven help us) punish Yisrael for not fulfilling their duties, while He impoverishes those nations that help Yisrael maintain their sinful ways.

[51] **Through orphans' funds** – Helping orphans is a holy pursuit. He that watches over orphan's funds that their estate may grow and prosper, acts like a father to the orphans. This is no mean achievement; we find that Hashem crowns Himself with the title 'Father of orphans,' (Tehillim 68.6). Still, if a person does this to enrich himself, he spoils the mitzva.

Hashem therefore, takes this one step further. Since He does not want people to do such holy mitzvos for money, but rather with pure motivations, He implants this rule in the world – When a person does such a mitzva for money, it does not enrich him.

[52] **See no success** – While one who pursues mitzvos becomes rich, the riches of the mitzvos themselves, are not in this world (Chulin 142a). None, except the most wicked of people may convert them into the currency of this world.

However, there are certain mitzvos that our world has turned into business ventures, enterprises that earn handsome profits. One such mitzva is shechita. Another is writing sifrei Torah, tefillin and mezuzos. However here too, Hashem has no wish that money-making motives tarnish this holy pursuit. Therefore, He makes a rule that such 'businesses' should not enjoy financial success.

[53] **They would stop writing** – Surely we already mentioned that wages that come from writing do not lead to financial success; why then these twenty-four fasts? – We may say that while there was little worry that scribes would become rich from

their craft, Still, our Rabbis were concerned that they may become wealthy through other means. This too, would cause them to stop writing. They therefore prayed and fasted that no scribe should become rich – through any enterprise!

CHAPTER FOURTEEN
PITFALLS

Eating your World

Our Rabbis teach that the reward for a mitzva is not in this world. (Chulin 142a) In truth, this entire world is too small to hold the reward of even one mitzva. Still, there are times when Hashem wishes to pay off those who are His enemies, that He may eradicate them from the world-to-come. Therefore He offers this enemy wealth in this world. If he accepts the offer, a deal is struck.[1]

> R' Elazar b'Rebbi Tzadok taught: To what may we compare the righteous in this world? To a tree that stands on pure ground, but part of its foliage hangs over impure ground. However, once this foliage has been pruned, it stands fully on pure ground. In this way Hashem brings sufferings on the righteous in this world, that they may inherit the world-to-come ...
>
> And to what may we compare the wicked in this world? To a tree that stands on impure ground, but part of its foliage hangs over pure ground. Once this foliage has been pruned, all of it stands on impure ground; Thus, Hashem grants goodness to the wicked in this world, that He may bankrupt them and place them in the lowest levels [of Gehinom], as the verse says: "There is a path that appears straight to men, but its end leads to death." (Mishle 14.12) (Kiddushin 40b)

Just as Hashem punishes the wicked in the world-to-come for the lightest sins, so He punishes the righteous in *this* world for their lightest sins. And just as Hashem rewards the righteous in the world-to-come for the

---

[1] **A deal is struck** – Still, we may ask, if the sum of the world's pleasures is too small to pay the reward for even one mitzva, how may Hashem compensate the wicked in this world? He is not giving them full value.

We may answer that there is an element of this world, more precious than the anything the next world can offer. This is life itself. While the time a person spends here may be trying and painful, still it affords him a fabulous treasure. This is the ability to serve Hashem of his own free will. Thus, when Hashem extends a wicked person's life, He pays him off in this world. (Vilna Gaon, quoted in Ohr haMussar vol. 2, p. 124)

smallest *mitzva*, so He rewards the wicked in this world for the smallest *mitzva*. (Taanis 11a)

Rav Pinchas said: Anyone who does a *mitzva*, and wishes to receive its reward immediately,[2] will not emerge clean from the wickedness and evil of this world. [Moreover] he is wicked and evil, and ultimately, leaves *nothing* for his children. (VaYikra Raba 36.3)

Rav Siemon said: Hashem, so to speak, said to our forefathers, "Here is a sack, here is money, here are My vaults. Take as much as you want."

However, had our fore-fathers taken the rewards for their lightest *mitzvos*, their children [as a result of their many failings] would have had no merit to sustain them. (ibid.)

Trade-offs

The wicked Nebuchnezer once did a mitzva through which he merited to become king over the whole world, as well as amassing the most magnificent wealth. While the mitzva was small, its reward was great; Hashem paid him off in this world.

Baladan, king of Babylon, after hearing of the great miracle Hashem had performed for King Chizkiyahu, wished to send him greetings and a gift. He wrote to him: Peace to you, King Chizkiyahu; peace to the city, Yerushalayim; peace to the Great G-d.

Nebuchnezer then was Baladan's chief scribe. He was not present when the king dictated this letter. Shortly afterwards, he came in and inquired after the contents of the letter. They told him how they had written it.

"You call him 'the Great G-d,'" he exclaimed, "and you place His Name at the end?!

"Rather you must write: 'Peace to you Great G-d; peace to the city, Yerushalayim; peace to King Chizkiyahu.'"

"You do it," they told him.

---

[2] **He wishes to receive its reward immediately** – While a person must trust that Hashem will reward him faithfully for all his mitzvos, still he should serve Him only for the privilege of serving Him, and not for any other reward.

What then if there is something that a person needs, something that he must ask of Hashem? – The answer to this is that he should ask, and ask. He should pray to Hashem for all he needs, but only as an appeal to His generosity, only as a favor and a gift. However, he should never demand it as his just desert, as a reward for his mitzvos. (See Rashi, Devarim 3.23)

He then ran four steps after the letter.[3] (Sanhedrin 96a)

Rejoice young man in your youth, feel good in your prime, walk in the ways of your heart and your eyes, *but know* that on all these things Hashem will judge you. (Koheles 11.9)

R' Yosef, son of R' Yehoshua, weakened and died. Shortly afterwards however, his soul returned to his body, and he recovered.

"What did you see in the next world?" his father asked him.

"It's an upside down world," he answered, those who are above here in this world [the wealthy] are below there, while those who are below here [the poor] are above there."

"No, my son," his father commented, "it is a true, clear world that you saw."[4] (Bava Basra 10b)

The wicked flourish like grass and the evildoers blossom – [only] that they may be destroyed for eternity. (Tehillim 92.8)

The tribes of Gad and Reuven were wealthy, they had much livestock, and they loved their money; so they dwelt outside *Eretz Yisrael*.[5] Thus, they were first of the tribes to be exiled...

_____

[3] **Four steps** – or, in other versions, three steps. (Tora Ore, Maharsha)
With his steps Nebuchadnezer glorified Hashem; however, he was an exceptionally perverse and evil man. Hashem therefore rewarded him – with a command and glory that made him king of the world – in his lifetime.
This event carries such an important lesson, that we allude to it three times each day. This is: The steps Nebuchadnezer took, gave him a power that he eventually used to destroy the first Beis haMikdash. We therefore, create an opposite spiritual force: As we take three steps back at the end of our prayer, we pray to Hashem that He speedily rebuild the Beis haMikdash, in our days. (Maharsha)
[4] **It is a true, clear world** – It is specifically this world that is the world of illusion, a world that masks the truth and deceives us. For it is only here that we fail to see Hashem; it is only here that the wicked achieve wealth and prestige; it is only here that the righteous suffer.
However, those who live in a Torah environment, have a better access to reality. Thus, the Gemara there continues:
"And how do we, the Torah scholars, appear in that world?" his father asked.
"Just as we are important down here," his son answered, "so we are important up there." (ibid.)
[5] **They dwelt outside** Eretz Yisrael – Although Moshe conquered the East side of the Jordan, this was not a part of Eretz Yisrael proper. Still, when the tribes of Gad and Reuven saw the large fertile plains of these lands – rich country that would generously nurture their huge herds and flocks, they were swayed to live there.

What caused them to separate from their brothers? – Their wealth. (BaMidbar Raba 22.7)

Despised are the wealthy[6] who love their money more than their souls.[7] (Tikunei Zohar 4)

Material Maladies

"Vanity of vanities ... all is vanity."[8] (Koheles 1.1)

I looked to all the acts I had done, all the labors I had labored – it was all in vain, an aggravation of the spirit; there is no profit under the sun.[9] (Koheles 2.11)

Sweet is the sleep of the laborer, whether he eats little or much, but *the rich man's gluttony* will not let him sleep.[10] (Koheles 5.11)

R' Eliezer told his students: Do not lay your trust in wealth. (Tana d'Bei Eliyahu Zuta 24)

He who trusts in his wealth,[11] will fall. (Mishle 11.28)

There is an evil I have seen under the sun ... a man that Hashem gives him wealth, property and honor, until nothing that his soul may desire does he lack – yet Hashem does not allow him to eat of it; a stranger consumes it. (Koheles 6.1,2)

However, since they followed their eyes and not their minds, they ultimately, paid a high price for their greed.

[6] **Despised are the wealthy** – The Heaven bans such people from entering the world-to-come.

[7] **More than their souls** – Instead of sacrificing monetary gain for the merit of mitzvos, they do the opposite – they sacrifice the merit of mitzvos for monetary gain.

[8] **All is vanity** – If a man as great and wealthy as Shlomo haMelech, tells us the everything in this world is vanity, surely we should take his words to heart. Similarly, when he tells us that the only reward of worth, is the reward a person gains through serving Hashem, we should listen attentively! We should realize that this alone is the best of all profits. (From Orchos Tzaddikim, introduction)

[9] **Under the sun** – i.e., in this world.

[10] **Will not let him sleep** – While the hardships of the poor are obvious, the wealthy also suffer in this world. Thus, the gains they 'enjoy' over their poor relatives are not that great. Moreover, their problems are a source of shame; for they are self-made.

[11] **He who trusts in his wealth** – When a person invests his trust in anything besides Hashem, he gives strength to the powers of impurity and evil. These gradually, invade his life, destroying all that is blessed and good.

Losing Control

The Mishna teaches: If on Shabbos, a person's house catches alight, he may save food enough for the three meals.

"Let him save more," the *Gemara* asks, "surely he is not profaning the Shabbos?"

"A person panics regarding his money," said Rava, "and if we allow him to take more, he may come to put out the fire." (Shabbos 117b)

The *Mishna* teaches: One who is still on the road when Shabbos enters, may ask a non-Jew to carry his purse for him.

"Why," asks the *Gemara*, "do the Rabbis permit him this? [Surely it goes against Rabbinic law?]"

"A person cannot restrain himself, when it comes to losing money," the Gemara answers, "if we do not permit him this, he may come to carry it himself, [a much greater prohibition]." (Shabbos 153a)

Money Mad

The wicked who chase after money, do so in vain. First they lose their minds, and eventually they even lose their wealth; it all ends up in the laps of the righteous.

The rich man thinks he is wise, but the poor man with insight, catches him out. (Mishle 28.11)

R' Tanchuma taught: Nebuchadnezer gathered *all* the world's wealth. He was however, so mean that as he was dying, he declared that he would leave none of his great wealth to his son, Eville. He therefore had great ships of copper built, filled them up with his wealth, and sank them in the Euphrates.[12] (Esther Raba 2.1)

However...

The very day that Koresh, a succeeding king, decreed that the [second] *Beis haMikdash* be built, Hashem revealed their hiding-place to him.[13] (ibid.)

"All the rivers flow into the sea, yet the sea is never full... " (Koheles 1.7)

---

[12] **And sank them in the Euphrates** – His money and power warped his thinking to such a degree, that he would not allow even his son to enjoy his great wealth.

[13] **Hashem revealed their hiding-place** – Koresh had brought honor to Hashem, and so Hashem honored him. We see here that Hashem manipulates every world event – all to fulfill His Great Divine Plan.

R' Shmuel bar Chova taught in the name of R' Acha that this verse refers to Rome: All moneys go to the Roman government, yet the Roman government is never sated; as R' Levi said, just as "a man's eyes are never filled" (Mishle 27.20), so the eyes of Rome are never filled ...

However, lest you think that once the moneys go to Rome, their owners never see them again, the verse therefore teaches:

"...and from there they return" (Koheles 1.7), from where the moneys gather in the present world, they are redistributed to the righteous in the days of Moshiach. (Koheles Raba 1.9)

Haman's wealth[14] was apportioned into three parts, a third went to Torah scholars, a third to Mordechai and Ester, and a third towards the building the *Beis haMikdash*. (Shocher Tov, Tehillim 78)

There is a man who lives alone, with no friend, no son, no brother, and he labors endlessly – yet his eyes are not satisfied with his wealth. [Let him ask himself,] for whom do I labor and destroy myself? – This too is a vanity and an evil business. (Koheles 4.8)

R' Yudan said in the name of R' Aivu: No man leaves the world with even half of his desires fulfilled, if he has one hundred, he wants two hundred; if he has two hundred,[15] he wants four hundred. (Koheles Raba 1.13)

Rav Leizer taught: Lot who dwelt in Sodom for the sake of his money, left with his hands on his head.[16] (Yerushalmi Sanhedrin 10)

Arrogance

When a person is wealthy, many evils tempt him. He feels that he need no longer trust in Hashem; he need no longer keep His mitzvos; he need no longer treat others with dignity and respect.

---

[14] **Haman's wealth** – Haman was the wealthiest man of his time. Still, this did not help him. He was hanged, and his property was transferred to his greatest enemies.

[15] **If he has two hundred** – His material possessions are unable to sate him and bring him happiness. Since he always needs more, he remains a needy man.

[16] **With his hands on his head** – When money brings a person to sin, when it is the agent that causes him to stray, Hashem then takes it away from him.

Lot went to Sodom, a place filled with wicked, evil people, to ensure and further his wealth. This move however, lead to his downfall. It distanced him from his uncle, Avraham, as well as Avraham's righteous ways. In this way it distanced him from Hashem. The Heavens therefore ruled that the wealth that had brought him to sin, should be taken from him.

The rich man's wealth is the city of his power,[17] and his arrogance is a high wall[18] around it. (Mishle 18.11)

"Wealth that brings its owner to evil." (Koheles 5.12). This verse, taught Reish Lakish, refers to Korach's wealth,[19] which brought him to pride,[20] and thereafter destroyed him. (Pesachim 119a, Rashi there)

The pauper pleads, and the rich man answers brazenly. (Mishle 18.23)

Still, pride is not only a problem for the high and mighty. It is also a sickness that afflicts the poor...

People hate an arrogant pauper.[21] (Pesachim 113b)

Warnings

Be careful ... lest you eat and are sated, you build good houses and dwell in them, your herd and flock increases, you accumulate gold and silver, your assets grow ... your heart becomes haughty,[22] and you forget Hashem, your Lord ... (Devarim 8.11,14)

---

[17] **The city of his power** – As opposed to the tzaddik, whose power and strength come only from Hashem. (Malbim)

[18] **His arrogance is a high wall** – In his imagination a high wall protects him. However, the protection that wealth provides, is a mirage. (Malbim)

[19] **Korach's wealth** – It lead him to one of the biggest mistakes in history, a rebellion against Hashem's greatest prophet, Moshe Rabbeinu.

[20] **Which brought him to pride** – A feeling of importance is one step away from pride, and two steps from evil. While a sense of self-worth is positive and good, while it helps a person build great, imposing structures, still there is a danger inherent in it. This is that it may lead to pride – one of the worst of all attributes.

Korach possessed a very great wealth. Unfortunately, this swayed him into thinking that he should be the Kohen Gadol, if not the leader of Yisrael. He therefore rebelled against Moshe Rabbeinu, an act that destroyed him and his followers – in this world, and the next!

[21] **People hate an arrogant pauper** – In a certain way, when a poor man is proud, his difficulties multiply. Since he has little reason to feel proud, he is even more ridiculous in others' eyes, and more of an abomination. Moreover, he imprisons himself in his poverty. For every person needs to get on with others (Kesuvos 17a) – especially one who is poor. Therefore, if he wishes to change his lot and enjoy some comfort and prosperity, he must rid himself of this evil attribute.

[22] **Your heart becomes haughty** – A person who possesses wealth, must ensure that it remains a good, positive, healthy wealth and does not chas v'shalom, enhance the forces of evil. How may he do this? Only with special preparations. He

Beware ... lest you declare to yourself, "My strength, and the power of my hands made me this wealth. Remember Hashem your Lord, for *it is He* who gives you strength to produce wealth. (Devarim 8.11,17,18)

No one may regard himself rich[23] before He who commands the world's creation. (Yerushalmi Peah 4.1)

Do not strut in front of a king. (Mishle 25.6)

The Price of Wealth

While the path of poverty is certainly a bitter path, wealth is not without its test – the prime test being the test of haughtiness. And the most bitter of fruits that comes from such pride is that a person in his affluence and satiety, may chas v'shalom deny Hashem. Maybe for this reason, Shlomo haMelech, the wisest of men, prayed that Hashem save him from the test of wealth.

Give me neither poverty, nor wealth[24] – feed me only my daily meal – that I should not be sated and deny Hashem, saying, Who is Hashem? Nor that I should be poor, steal, and swear falsely. (Mishle 30.8,9)

Kevulos refers to lambs whose sexual organs have been covered over. Why are they called kevulos?

---

must have the right set of priorities, and then live by them. The first of these priorities is humility.

[23] **No one may regard himself rich** – One who has much money may feel superior to others. This feeling however, is foolishness. For such a person forgets the One who commanded the creation of all – and to not know Hashem, is to not know anything.

What then should the wealthy man think? – "All that I possess is only mine on deposit. I must look after it properly, and use it responsibly. For ultimately, I will have to account for every penny of it. I will have to answer the question: Did I spend Heaven's money for Heaven's sake, or not?"

[24] **Neither poverty, nor wealth** – It would seem that Hashem did not listen to Shlomo's prayer; after all, he was one of the wealthiest of men who ever lived. How can this be?

We may say though, that Hashem did listen to his prayer. What Shlomo really wanted is that Hashem protect him from the test of wealth, and Hashem did just this. He helped Shlomo use his wealth for the glory of Hashem and the Jewish people. Moreover, He aided Shlomo to become a model of piety and heavenly wisdom, as well as a prophet. Thus, He saved him from wealth!

Another thought: Once Shlomo himself appreciated the danger inherent in wealth, and could ask to be spared of it, he was ready to receive it in abundance.

Rav Huna said, "Since they cannot have offspring, they are like people loaded (kevul) with silver and gold, who are pampered and do no work. They too do not produce fruit."[25] (Shabbos 54a)

Ilfa and R' Yochanan learnt Torah in extreme poverty; once, when their situation was especially pressing, they declared, "Let us engage in business, that we may fulfill the verse, "There shall be no poverty amongst you."[26] (Devarim 15.4)

Later the Gemara relates, R' Yochanan changed his mind ...

"I am returning," R' Yochanan told Ilfa, "and rather fulfill the verse, "There will always be paupers in the land" (ibid.) R' Yochanan returned; Ilfa did not return.

Later, when Ilfa returned, R' Yochanan had already been appointed Rosh haYeshiva. "Had you been here," the students told Ilfa, "you, and not R' Yochanan would have been Rosh haYeshiva.[27] (Taanis 21a)

---

[25] **They too do not produce fruit** – One of the problems wealth leads to is inactivity and sluggishness. For when a person feels he has all he needs, he no longer strives for anything; he no longer produces fruit.

What is the solution to his problem? – To stop feeling rich and begin feeling poor. Let him ask himself: "While I may have much money, do I have friends? And while I may have many friends, do I have mitzvos? Am I a master over the Torah, or even a part of it? Have I acquired good attributes – am I kind and considerate; do I help others? Am I righteous, pious, humble? Do I have prophecy? Am I close to Hashem?"

Just as a person must appreciate all he has, so he must appreciate all that he lacks. Only in this way, may he reach new heights. Only with this awareness, may he acquire a true and full wealth.

[26] **Let us engage in some business** – While wealth or poverty is a function of good fortune, it is also affected by the hard work a person does. Sometimes, when a person's lot is to suffer poverty, he may well change this by entering the working world.

[27] **Had you been here** – A person must exercise caution when he seeks to change his lot. Had Ilfa returned with Rebbi Yochanan, it is he and not Rebbi Yochanan, who would have received the crown of Rosh haYeshiva. Also this position would have bettered his financial situation.

However, since he was hasty, he remained Ilfa. He received no special place in Jewish history. Rebbi Yochanan on the other hand, went on to become one of history's most prominent scholars and leaders.

CHAPTER FIFTEEN

TRUE WEALTH

Whose wealth is it?

The earth and all its contents, are Hashem's, the inhabited world and all who dwell in it; He founded it on the seas; He prepared it by the rivers ... (Tehillim 24.1,2)

You remembered the earth and watered it, greatly enriching it ... You prepare their grain ... You water their furrows, satisfying its peoples; You soften [the earth] with showers, You bless its growth; You crown the year with Your goodness and Your paths drip with abundance. (Tehillim 65.10,11,12)

They all look to You with hope, to provide them with food at the right time ... You open Your hand and sate them with goodness; [but] when You hide Your face, they panic.[1] (Tehillim 104.27-29)

When you gather in their spirit, they die, and return to their dust.[2] (Tehillim 104.29)

He gives food to all flesh, for His kindness is forever.[3] (Tehillim 136.25)

Who then is rich?

There are many ways of measuring wealth. A person may be the most powerful of men, and count himself wealthy; or he can have three more potatoes than his next-door neighbor, and consider himself wealthy. This is the definition our Rabbis give us:

Who is a wealthy man? One who's townsmen honor him for his wealth.[4] (Kidushin 49b)

---

[1] **They panic** – For You, and You alone, are their source of sustenance.

[2] **To their dust** – The spirit of life that permeates every living being, is a spark of Hashem Himself. Thus, when he reclaims it, they must collapse.

[3] **His kindness is forever** – Hashem besides giving His creatures life, also gives them His intrinsic goodness, His compassion and mercy.

[4] **One who's townsmen honor him** – We learn from this that wealth is defined as the esteem other people give the person. This in effect, is what the person who toils for wealth, receives.

Who is a wealthy man? R' Tarfon said: One who owns one hundred vineyards, one hundred fields and one hundred slaves to work them. (Shabbos 25b)

Still ...

R' Yochanan said: There is one who is rich in the street and poor at home;[5] there is one who is rich at home and poor in the street; as the verse says, "There are wealthy men with nothing, and poor men with great fortunes. (Mishle 13) (Yerushalmi Shavuos 7.2)

Monetary Limits

Three things a person loves in his life time, one of them is his wealth...[6]

At the time of his death, he gathers all money and properties and says to them, "I invested so much effort into you; day and night I worried about you; please save me from this death!"

"Did you not learn," his riches answer, "that 'wealth does not help in a day of anger[7]' (Mishle 11.4)." (Pirkei d'R' Eliezer 34)

Don't panic when you see another growing rich, when the glory of his house increases. He will not take it all with him when he dies – his glory will not descend with him. (Tehillim 49.17,18)

Better off is the poor man who walks honestly, than the crooked man who is rich. (Mishle 28.6)

---

[5] **Rich in the street and poor at home** – There are two types of wealth; one is a superficial wealth, he who is 'rich in the street'; the other, a real wealth, he who is 'rich at home.'

While everyone easily realizes that real wealth is better than apparent wealth, still we see an interesting phenomenon. This is that the majority of people favor apparent wealth over real wealth. They prefer flashy cars, fashionable dress and exotic holidays, to money in the bank. As ridiculous as this sounds, one who examines his world, will see that this is so. And why? – We must say that since they are too lazy to think through their priorities, they lose sight of true values, as they rush after the crowds.

At a deeper level, 'rich in the street' refers to one who has great material wealth, while 'rich at home' refers to one who has spiritual wealth. Here too, most people will agree that to be 'rich at home' is preferable to 'rich in the street.' Yet, again, we find the same phenomenon: People throw eternal wealth out the window, as they madly chase after riches that may last no more than a lifetime.

[6] **One of them** – The other two are his family and his good deeds. (ibid.)

[7] **Wealth does not help** – Only a person's good deeds are able to help him in the next world.

Other Standards

There are different types of wealth. Some of them however, are just not worth having.

Rav Papa taught: There is none as poor as a dog;[8] there is none as rich as a pig.[9] (Shabbos 155b)

What then, is the ideal form of wealth? One requirement should be that it outlasts our temporal, physical, limited realm. Here are some more ideas from our Rabbis...

Who is a wealthy man? R' Akiva said: One whose wife conducts herself in pleasant ways. (Shabbos 25b)

A good name is better than great wealth, and the affection of others,[10] better than silver and gold. (Mishle 22.1)

Children are a legacy from Hashem; they are the reward of the womb.[11]

Like a warrior's arrows, are the children of one's youth.

Fortunate is the man who fills his quiver with them.[12] (Tehillim 127.3-5)

"And Yitzchak prayed (veya'atir) ... " (Breishis 25.21) R' Yochanan explained this, that he poured out his prayers richly (atir).[13] (Breishis Raba 63.5)

---

[8] **As poor as a dog** – A dog has much difficulty finding its food. The Gemara relates that for this reason Hashem was especially kind to the dog; He created him with an intestinal system that holds its food for three days. Thus, he does not starve in his poverty.

[9] **As rich as a pig** – A pig is able to eat anything. Furthermore, his master feeds him very well! And since all he wants of life is to eat well, there is none as contented and rich as he!

Here is something to think about. When the Gemara declares that none is as rich as a pig, this means that there is no other being in all of Creation as rich as him. He is wealthier even than the wealthiest billionaires. The question then becomes, would anyone willingly, happily, exchange places with a pig? Even if he was a dog, would he agree to be a pig? No? Why not? (Rav Simcha Zissel of Kelm, Chochma v'Mussar)

[10] **The affection of others** – Money does not buy love. Likewise it doesn't buy the true respect of others.

[11] **The reward of the womb** – Human fruits are much more precious than any material wealth.

[12] **The man who fills his quiver** – Just as there is power in large numbers, so does a member of a large family enjoy an extraordinary blessing. Likewise, the person who gathers many loyal friends and students, enjoys a special prosperity.

Rav Dimi said: Hillel and Shavna were brothers; Hillel toiled in Torah [in great poverty – *Rashi*], and Shavna was a businessman.

One day Shavna said to Hillel, "Come let us pool our riches and split them."

At this a heavenly voice called out: Even if a man gives all the wealth of his house for his love [of Torah], they will ridicule him.[14] (Shir haShirim 8.8) (Sota 21a)

King Moenbaz[15] generously distributed the wealth of his treasuries, and his ancestors' treasuries, in the years of famine. His brothers and family came to protest.

"Your fathers stashed away wealth and added to what their fathers had left them, and you squander it all?!" they said.

My fathers stashed away wealth below," Moenbaz answered, "while I stash it away above. My fathers hoarded it in a place where others may take it from them, while I hoard it in a place where no hand touches it. My fathers saved a wealth that produces no profits, while I save a wealth that produces profits.[16] My fathers accumulated material riches, while I accumulate lives.[17] My fathers gathered in wealth for others, while I gather in wealth for myself. My fathers collected in this world, while I collect in the world-to-come.[18] (Bava Basra 11a)

---

[13] **He poured out his prayers richly** – Wealth enters every aspect of our lives. There is always a better way, a richer way of doing things. To 'live richly,' we must think and act richly. Our forefather, Yitzchok, was such a man. He had a fabulous material wealth. In his time, people said they would rather have the dung of his livestock, than all of King Avimelech's silver and gold. (Rashi, Breishis 26.13)

Here we learn that Yitzchok's wealth extended beyond the physical. It entered his behavior and his entire spiritual realm – his 'prayer was rich.' This certainly helped him become who he was, a father of the Jewish people and one of the greatest people who ever lived.

[14] **They will only ridicule him** – No riches match the Torah's wealth, even when they are given with love. Its influence penetrates right through Creation. Its glory radiates in every world.

[15] **King Moenbaz** – son of Queen Heleni, of the Chashmonean family. (Rashi)

[16] **A wealth that produces profits** – These are the 'fruits' of the mitzva. While the principle reward of a mitzva awaits a person in the next world, he may enjoy in the fruits in the here and now. (Rashi)

[17] **I accumulate lives** – With my charities I save the lives of the poor; and Thus, I gain merit of giving them life.

[18] **I collect in the world-to-come** – Ask anyone: Would you prefer an hour of wealth and a thousand years of poverty, or an hour's poverty and a thousand years

Who has wealth?

Certain people need certain things before they can feel rich. Obviously the more 'spoilt' they are, the more they need. However, the Rabbis do point to certain items as especially defining wealth – items that are, in a sense, EVERYTHING!

"You will be blessed in the city..." (Devarim 28.3)

"This means," said Rav, "that your house will be close to the *shul*."

R' Yochanan said: "It means that your bathroom fixtures are near to your dining-room table."[19] (Bava Metzia 107a)

"You will be blessed in the field..." (Devarim 28.3)

This means, said Rav, "that your fields are close to the city."

R' Yochanan said, "It means that your crops are threefold;[20] one-third is grain; one-third, olives; and one-third, grapes. " (ibid.)

"...you will be blessed as you enter and you will be blessed as you leave. (Devarim 28.5)

"This means," said R' Yochanan, "that your exit from this world, will be like your entrance. Just as your entrance is without sin, so your exit will be without sin.[21] (ibid.)

"And it will be that if you do not listen to Hashem, your G-d, to observe and fulfill all His commands ... and you will serve the enemies Hashem sends you, in hunger, thirst, nakedness and lacking all ... ," (Devarim 28.48);

---

of wealth? Even the simplest person would answer that a thousand years of wealth, is a good trade-off for a little misery. Similarly, every person should agree that an investment he makes in eternity, is better than any investment he makes in this temporary world.

[19] **Near to your dining-room table** – In early days, a person had to put on a coat and boots, and take a lamp with him to the toilet. Even the richest men and their elegant wives, had to undertake this trek. How wealthy then are we today who have the benefits of modern plumbing.

Similarly a person should notice every convenience and comfort that is a part of his world, and feel grateful and 'more wealthy' for it.

[20] **Your crops are threefold** – Thus, if one crop is blighted, the other crops will still sustain their owner. This insurance, as with any insurance, is a form of wealth. Similarly, one who has a full trust in Hashem, has a very great wealth. For can there be a great insurer than Hashem?

[21] **Your exit will be without sin** – This ultimately is the greatest wealths of all. Happy will be the person who achieves this!

What, asks the Gemara, does 'lacking all' refer to?[22]

- Rav Ami said in the name of Rav: He has no lamp and no table.[23]
- Rav Chisda said: He has no wife.[24]
- Rav Sheishes said: He has no one to serve him.[25]
- Rav Nachman said: He lacks insight and knowledge.
- A *Breisa* teaches: He lacks salt and oil.[26]

---

[22] **What does 'lacking all' refer to?** – In other words, the verse has already stated that he suffers from hunger, thirst and no roof over his head. What then does the word "all" refer to?

[23] **No lamp and no table** – A person who lives without a lamp and a table, lives like an animal. Once he is denied the distinction he enjoys over lower creatures, he lacks all.

This is especially true for a Torah scholar. For if he has no lamp or table, how may he learn at night? (R' Barak Bar-Chaim)

[24] **No wife** – See Chapter Nine.

[25] **No one to serve him** – A servant is one of the heights of luxury. How can Rav Sheishes say that one who lacks a servant 'lacks all'?

A rich man who loses his wealth, forgets over time the grandeur that was once his. Rather, he worries more about his immediate needs, food, shelter, etc. He has few thoughts to spare on the luxuries he once enjoyed. If someone asked him, "Do you miss the splendor you once had?" he would look at him with surprise. (Beis haLevi, Parshas Shmos.) However since this loss is a loss of his original identity, he has lost 'his all.'

The Jewish people too, are a very grand people – Sons of Kings. (Shabbos 67a). As servants of the King of all kings, and Master of all Creation, they are really a very elevated, noble people. Their place is at the heights of society. However, since they have lived for so long without the honor that is theirs, the thought of equating their lack of servants with a 'lack of all' seems strange, and almost comical.

May Hashem return us soon to Himself...and renew our days, as the days of old. (Eicha 5.21)

[26] **Salt and oil** – While a person may have bread and potatoes, if he lacks salt and oil, he 'lacks all.' Salt adds flavor to our foods; oil gives the person a feeling of satisfaction. Without these, a person will not enjoy or derive full benefit from his food.

Just as a person needs salt in his food, so he needs a purpose for living, a reason to get up in the morning. This adds flavor to his every day, a lust for life. To find such a spice, a person must learn Torah. Only this can give his life real purpose. Likewise, just as a person needs oil in his food, so he needs to taste success; he needs to see the fruits of his labors. Tasting such success, smoothens over the stress he faces each day. It allows him to enjoy his life. However, when he faces failure after failure, this breaks him and destroys his life. To see success, a person must

Abaye said: The only pauper is the one who lacks insight and knowledge.

In *Eretz Yisrael* they say: If he has this (insight and knowledge), he has everything; but if he doesn't have this, what does he have? If he acquires this, what does he lack; but if he does not acquire this, what has he acquired?! (Nedarim 41a)

Happy is the man who finds wisdom ... it is better to deal in this than to deal in silver, and its profits are fine gold; it is more precious than pearls, and all your possessions may not equal it.[27] (Mishle 3.13-15)

A pauper is one poor in Torah and *mitzvos*; for only Torah and *mitzvos* are ones wealth. (Zohar, Shmos 93)

Fulfilled Living

The secret of true wealth is a secret of acquiring the right attitudes. Why is it a secret? Because even though it stares every single person in the face, most people fail to see it.

Death is common, wealth is not.

Rav Papa said: This fits the folk-saying, "If they tell you your friend has died, believe it; but if they tell you he has become rich, don't believe it."[28] (Gitin 30b)

Alexander (the Great) of Macedon, asked the Rabbis of the South ten questions. One was: Who is rich?

He who is happy with his lot, they replied. (Tamid 32a)

Who is rich? – He who derives satisfaction from his wealth.[29] (Yerushalmi Peah 4.2)

---

merit Heaven's help. Toiling all day, every day, is not enough. If Hashem will not bless his efforts, he will not succeed.

Thus, one who lacks purpose (the salt of life), as well as the sensation of success (oil that lubricates him), lacks all.

[27] **All your possessions may not equal it** – Wisdom has eternal value. It enriches the one who owns it in this world, and the next!

[28] **Don't believe it** – Becoming wealthy is not like dying. Everyone eventually dies. It is a natural phenomenon. However, acquiring riches requires initiative, prayer and labor. It is not the product of good fortune, but rather of toil. And when one defines wealth as possessing the right attitudes, it then becomes even harder to acquire. There is no simple formula that ensures such a wealth.

[29] **Satisfaction from his wealth** – A 'needy' person is someone who needs. He may have millions of dollars, but if he needs more, he is still in need. Only when he is

Is the pauper not the one who thinks 'poorly'; and is not the wealthy man the one who thinks 'richly'?[30] (Kesuvos 68a)

Ben Zoma, on seeing large groups of people, would declare: "Blessed are You, Hashem, who has created all these people to serve me ...

"How hard *Adam haRishon* had to toil to eat bread; he had to plow, sow, reap, gather in the harvest, thresh, winnow, sort, grind, sift, knead and bake. Only after all this, could he eat. I, on the other hand, wake up in the morning, and find everything ready.

"How hard *Adam haRishon* had to toil before he had a garment to wear; he had to shear, bleach, comb, spin, weave, and only then did he have what to wear. I, however, wake up in the morning, and find it all ready.

---

satisfied with what he has, when he doesn't 'need' anything, then he is rich. If he is happy with his lot, then he is wealthy.

It would seem however, that no person can be absolutely rich. He cannot be totally self-sufficient. While he may own much money, he still needs others. He needs their support, physically and emotionally. He needs people to work in his businesses, and to honor and respect him. Without all this, he is only half the person.

Therefore, a person may only think of himself as rich in terms of certain items, items such as money in the bank, the power to lead and influence others, etc. However, when it comes to other items – matters such as feelings of well-being, security and love – he must think of himself as poor.

Still, the question is, how can a person be wealthy regarding anything? Surely Hashem provides him with everything – the air he breathes, as well as the lungs with which to breathe it; food, water, shelter, friends, and the health to enjoy all this. Can he then be wealthy?!

One approach would be to convince himself that Hashem does not exist, chas v'shalom. Then, once he has 'nature,' he no longer 'needs' anything. This however, is not a real solution. For if he bases his wealth on a falsehood, he may only enjoy a false wealth!

We must say therefore, that a wealthy person is one who feels Hashem at his side, helping him and supporting him. If (1) he recognizes his lot – this is Hashem who makes him and takes him through his life, and (2) he accepts this – he serves Hashem with joy – then he is truly wealthy!

When a person recognizes that Hashem gives him everything, and with great kindness too, he comes to true wealth. For then he aligns himself with his Maker. He stands before His King, and lives in His palace. In a certain sense, he is even a part of the King Himself. At this point, he acquires access to the King's wealth; as our Rabbis hint to in their rich language: The slave of a King, is a king. (Shavuos 47b)

[30] **The one who thinks 'richly'** – All depends on a person's thoughts.

"People toil daily, and come right up to my door;[31] while I wake up in the morning and find everything ready." (Brochos 58a)

R' Chiya bar Abba taught in R' Yochanan's name: The Great Assembly [originally] ruled that people should say *havdala* in the evening prayer. However, when people became wealthy, they reenacted to say it over a cup of wine.[32] (Brochos 33a)

Take pleasure in Hashem, and He will give you your heart's desire.[33] (Tehillim 37.4)

Ultimately Equal

Rav Chisda taught: What does the verse "Praise Hashem...His kindness is for all" (Tehillim 136.1) teach? – That Hashem collects His debts with great kindness; an ox from the rich man, a lamb from the poor, an egg from the orphan[34] and a chicken from the widow.[35] (Pesachim 118a)

---

[31] **Up to my door** – Ben Zoma was a wealthy man. Therefore, all types of merchants, with all forms of business, would come to his door. (Rashi)

Ben Zoma however, was rich in a larger sense. He praised Hashem to the utmost. He developed an amazing sense of gratitude and appreciation, and would openly recognize the greatness of Hashem's gifts. This we must say, was his true wealth.

We too enjoy a wealth like Ben Zoma's. We have ready-baked bread at our bakeries, and ready-to-wear clothes at the local department store. Still, if we will not cultivate our gratitude, we lose our good fortunes!

[32] **Over a cup of wine** – Blessing Hashem over a cup of wine, is a more beautiful way of expressing appreciation for Hashem's great generosity. Thus, a person who can afford to bless Hashem over a cup of wine, should make this his duty.

Similarly in all situations, a person must use his wealth to serve Hashem. Only then, does he show true recognition for all Hashem gives him. Only then does he enjoy his wealth to the full. Moreover, once he appreciates his wealth correctly, this gives him access to an even greater wealth.

[33] **Your heart's desire** – When we express gratitude to Hashem for all He gives us, we treat our wealth correctly. Acknowledging our wealth puts it in 'its right place.' It shows that we know the value of our wealth. Moreover, Hashem may now entrust us with still greater wealth.

[34] **An egg from the orphan** – The Torah recognizes the intrinsic equality of all men. One who sins, must atone for the sin with a sacrifice. Yet while the sins may be the same, each person atones for it according to his financial standing; the rich man with an ox, the poor man with a lamb.

The idea here is that while people live on different societal planes, they all however, experience the same range of pleasure and pain, of reward and punishment.

Rich Forever

A person who must choose between the riches of this world and the wealth of the next, between prosperity that lasts seventy, eighty years, and that which lasts forever, will surely choose the latter. His first concern will be to build his home of the future.

> R' Chiya had a friend in Bashna. This friend made him a feast that could boast of every delicacy that came into being during the six days of Creation.
>
> "What will your G-d provide you with in the future," he asked R' Chiya," that is greater than this?"
>
> "Your meal," R' Chiya answered him, "must end,[36] but the feast Hashem will make for His righteous in the next world, is eternal. (Ester Raba 2.4)
>
> How great is the goodness You conceal[37] for those who hold You in awe. (Tehillim 31.20)
>
> Keep my mitzvos,[38] says Hashem...
>
> "...that it may be good for you and that you may enjoy length of days." (Devarim 5.16)

This then is the lesson: Striving for 'bigger' goals does not change the joys and frustrations a person must and will experience. Therefore, he should look for his happiness in the very place Hashem places him. And while all people need to constantly change and grow, to achieve greater successes, still he should work only in his own field. He should try to change that which Hashem challenges him to change. On the other hand, that which is unnatural to his self, he should leave alone. He will only become poorer and more miserable, when he chases it.

[35] **A chicken from the widow** – This does not speak only of sacrifices made in the Beis haMikdash, but also of those everyday losses that upset us all. The Rabbis indicate this when they refer to a chicken and an egg – items that are unfit for the altar. Thus, just as we are happy to give charity in times of trouble, so we must be grateful for such loses too. For through them we may atone for our sins.

[36] **Your meal must end** – People are limited beings and live limited lives; and so their pleasures too, are limited. Even their simplest joys – joys their finances and health easily afford them – they must eventually surrender.

[37] **The goodness You conceal** – No one may see the reward Hashem keeps for His righteous. It is so far beyond anything any person has ever experienced, that it defies imagination. Even the greatest prophets could not visualize it. (Based on Maharal; introduction to Gevuros Hashem)

[38] **Keep my mitzvos** – While this verse refers to 'honoring your parents,' the most difficult of the Torah's mitzvos, a similar wording appears by the mitzva of sending away the mother-bird, the easiest of the Torah's mitzvos. From this we learn that every mitzva has its roots in the next world. (Chulin 142a)

"That it may be good for you." Where? In the world that is all good.[39]

"...and that you may enjoy length of days." Where? In the world of eternity. (Kiddushin 39b)

R' Yakov said: This world is an entrance hall[40] before the next world; [therefore] prepare yourself in this entrance hall that you may enter the palace. (Avos 4.22)

R' Yakov said: Greater is one moment of pleasure in the world-to-come, than all the life of this world.[41] (Avos 4.17)

Even in this World

One the greatest challenges a man has, is to live with faith; to feel Hashem constantly at his side. Thus he lives in this world, as he will in the next; which is ultimately, the greatest wealth.

"Hashem blessed Avraham with all ..." (Breishis 24.1)

"I have eaten of all ... [Yitzchak said]" (Breishis 27.33)

"And Yakov said ... Hashem has been gracious to me, and I have all." (Breishis 33.10,11)

---

[39] **The world that is all good** – In this world, pain and discomfort accompany even the greatest of pleasures. However, the delights of eternity are all good.

[40] **An entrance hall** – A man once gave an architect the specifications of his new home. "Please ensure," he told him, "that my entrance hall is large and majestic."

"If I make the entrance large," the architect replied, "there will be little space left for your inner rooms."

Similarly, one who tries to squeeze too much pleasure from this world, short changes himself in the world-to-come. (Chafetz Chaim, Shem Olam, Part 2 ch.4)

The Chafetz Chaim also relates this parable: Once a wealthy wholesaler did business with a simple farmer. "Look here," he told the farmer, "for each sack of wheat I take, I will put one penny in this bottle, and at the end of the season, we will count the pennies, and accordingly, I will pay you for the sacks I took."

The farmer however, felt he would outsmart the wholesaler. Therefore, every so often he would steal a few of the pennies from the bottle. Had he thought for a moment though, he would have realized that he was only stealing from himself.

Similarly, one who instead of serving Hashem, 'steals' from this world's delights, short changes himself in the world-to-come.

[41] **All the life of this world** – Even if all the world's pleasures were concentrated, were gathered and squeezed into one single moment, still they would not equal the least delight, not even a whiff of pleasure, that is in the world-to-come. (See Michtav M'Eliyahu vol.1. p.4.)

From these verses our Rabbis taught, that Hashem gave our forefathers –
while they were yet in this world[42] – a taste of the world-to-come.[43] (Bava
Basra 17a)

---

[42] **While they were** yet **in this world** – We make a mistake to think that this world
and the next are two absolutely unconnected worlds. There is really only one
world. It is just that this world has not yet evolved into the Garden of Eden it is
destined to be ... Thus, if you want the afterlife to be an ultimate experience, you
must learn in which ways your present life contains elements of the 'Garden of
Eden' experience. (Rav Ezriel Tauber. See "As in Heaven, so on Earth" vol. 1,
chp.11)

[43] **A taste of the world-to-come** – Each one of the patriarchs had great material
wealth. However, their ability to taste the next world while still in this one, was
their true ALL.

CHAPTER SIXTEEN

LESSONS FROM HEAVEN

The forty years Yisrael spent in the desert serve as the foundation for our entire history. During this time they lived on the food that the angels themselves live on – Mann.

Heavenly Food

When Hashem took Yisrael out of Egypt, He required them to maintain the highest levels of trust and faith. Therefore He fed them mann, a marvelous, miraculous food that fell from the sky. Through the mann they learnt how to depend on Hashem's kindness for their survival.

What role does the mann play in our lives? It is an example and an omen. It is an example: It teaches us that we too may live as our mann-eating fathers lived; we too may reach the exalted spiritual levels they enjoyed. Also, it is an omen: Hashem may at times, insist that we live at a high level of faith, whether we want to or not. He may force us to live on miracles, miracles that come from one day to the next, even though we do not choose such a lifestyle for ourselves. Thus, it pays us to learn the lessons of the mann[1] very well!

> How would the *mann* fall? First the North wind would blow and sweep the desert; then the rain would fall and launder the ground; then dew would arise and a wind would blow through it, spreading it until it had an appearance of a shimmering gold table. Then the *mann* would fall.[2]
> (Mechilta 16.14)

---

[1] **The lessons of the mann** – As we approach the end of this work, let us remember that we cannot penetrate the depths of our Rabbis' brilliance, with one, or even two and three, easy reads. Rather, we must contemplate each teaching. We must look repeatedly for new ideas to light up our minds. Also, as we go through our everyday, we must remember these teachings, using them as a flashlight to expose the workings of our world. Only then, may we merit to be the 'students' of our glorious ancestors, the teachers and leaders of Yisrael.

[2] **Then the mann would fall** – A gift from Heaven is a heavenly gift; nothing can 'out-class' the Originator of all. Like the Rabbis, we too must learn to look for the beauty in all Hashem gives us. Moreover, we must also try to discover Hashem Himself from within His wondrous works.

R' Yosi b'Rebbi Chanina taught: When they found the *mann* it had dew below it and dew above it[3] – as though it was in a box. (Yoma 75a)

Rav Avahu said: A person could taste every type of food[4] in the *mann*. (ibid.)

R' Akiva said: Mann is a food that angels eat.[5]

R' Yishmael said: It is a food that is fully absorbed into man's 248 limbs; [he need never use the bathroom.[6]] (Yoma 75b)

R' Yosi b'Rebbi Chanina taught: For youths it was like bread, for elders it was like oil, and for infants it was like honey.[7] (ibid.)

---

[3] **Dew below, dew above** – The dew above formed a glistening wrap, adding to its freshness and beauty. The dew below, kept it appetizingly clean. The details of every gift Hashem gives us, have built into them His genius and glory. Not only are they technical marvels; they also display how Hashem caters to our psyche and emotions – He sends us His mann in ways that are honorable and attractive.

[4] **Every type of food** – Our Rabbis teach that whatever foodstuff a person focused on, he could taste in the mann. If he thought of that which was sweet, it was delectably sweet; if he thought of that which was bitter, it was caustically bitter. And what of the person who did not focus on anything? – For him, our Rabbis teach, the mann was tasteless. (Heard from Rav Shmuel Yitzchok Herman, shlita)

Similarly, each person has to focus on the beauty of his world, thereby adding taste to his life. It is up to him to inject his everyday with excitement, with the beauty and joy that Hashem hides into the folds of our every day. If, however, he does not inject his life with life – or worse, he injects it with poisonous thoughts – he fills his days with a cruel loneliness.

[5] **Food that angels eat** – Hashem by feeding them mann wished to show Yisrael that within this physical world, they may live on a spiritual plane. This lesson applies to us as well. When we search for spirituality within our very physical lifestyles, we also live on mann. Furthermore, we reach the heights our fathers did.

[6] **He need never use the bathroom** – As good as physical food may be, a part of it always goes to waste. The body rejects it. In the spiritual realm however, this is not so. For within the soul is a power that can convert every element of Creation, into pure holiness and energy.

Similarly, one who pursues physical pleasures always experiences some disappointment, some sadness. These are the waste products of his endeavors. However, when he aspires towards spirituality, then he may transform even the most dismal failures into fabulous profits.

[7] **For infants it was like honey** – Different people have different needs. Still, the mann could satisfy them all. Each person miraculously received exactly what he needed. Similarly, one who lives with spiritual goals, can see how Hashem always gives him exactly what he needs. Whether it is good, or not so good, it is always a springboard to greater heights.

The sweetness of honey is a sixtieth[8] of the *mann's* good taste. (Brochos 57b)

Rav Assi said: It was round like a seed, and shone white like a pearl.[9] (ibid.)

Rav Yehuda said in the name of Rav [or according to others, Rav Chama b'Rebbi Chanina said]: Women's perfumes came down with the *mann*. (ibid.)

Rav Chama said: Spices and seasonings came down with the *mann*.[10] (ibid.)

Rav Shmuel bar Nachmani said in the name of R' Yonason: Precious stones and pearls fell down with the *mann*.[11] (ibid.)

When the sun rose higher, it melted. (Shmos 16.21)

The molten mann would then form streams that flowed down to the sea; and wild deer, antelope and gazelle would drink it from these streams. Thus, the nations of the world who hunted these animals, would taste the mann that fell for Yisrael.[12] (Mechilta 16.23)

Day by Day

The mann teaches Yisrael the approach and attitude they should adopt concerning their livelihood. One such lesson is that since Hashem feeds us day by day, a person should not make excessive provisions for his future.

---

[8] **Honey is a sixtieth** – When a person enters the realm of the spirit, his physical limitations fall away. His consciousness expands many times over. He now perceives his world from very broad, beautiful perspectives. He appreciates life's joys on new, exalted levels.

A person who tasted mann, entered just such a realm. Thus, it gave him great delight. Likewise, one who learns Torah, prays with deep concentration or throws his whole self into helping others, enters this realm. By focusing his thoughts and drives on fulfilling Hashem's will, he enjoys a sensation similar to those who ate mann.

[9] **Like a pearl** – Our Rabbis sought the most beautiful of words to describe the mann's glory.

[10] **Women's perfumes...spices and seasonings...** – Hashem wished Yisrael to learn that every delight, is His to give or not give.

[11] **Precious stones and pearls fell down** – The mann contained every type of wealth, pleasure and satisfaction that may be found throughout Creation

[12] **The nations of the world ... would taste the** mann – and learn of Yisrael's greatness. Rashi Hashem allows others to see and taste of the glory He grants His tzaddikim. Perhaps then, they too will re-evaluate their lives, and change their ways.

Thus, instead of spending precious time worrying about his 'parnosa,' he should spend it more productively, i.e., to Torah study and acts of kindness.

"I am raining down bread from the Heavens..." [says Hashem,] "that I may test them,[13] will they follow My Torah or not." (Shmos 16.4)

"The people picked the day's needs on that day" (Devarim 16.4)

R' Elazar haModai said: This was so that they would not pick on one day for the next. He who created the day, created its sustenance.

Based on this R' Elazar would say: One who has bread in his basket and says, "What will I eat tomorrow?" lacks faith. (Mechilta 16.4)

R' Shimon taught: Why did the *mann* not come once a year? – This was so that *Yisrael* would direct their hearts to their heavenly Father.

The following parable illustrates this: Once there was a king who established a yearly allowance for his son. The son however, only came to visit his father when he came for his allowance. "Surely it's enough to see my father when he feeds me," he thought. Therefore the king decreed that he should receive a daily allowance.

Similarly with *Yisrael* – a man who had five sons or five daughters, sits and worries, "Maybe no *mann* will fall tomorrow, and we will all die of hunger. May it be Your will Hashem, that the *mann* will fall."

Thus, *Yisrael* would incline their hearts to their heavenly Father. (Sifri B'Ha'alosecha 89)

Moshe told them: Let no man leave over *mann* until the next morning ... and there were people who left it over to the next morning, and worms infested it,[14] and it rotted. (Shmos 16.19,20)

R' Shimon bar Yochai said: Only those who eat *mann* may penetrate the Torah's secrets.[15] (Mechilta 16.4)

---

[13] **That I may test them** – The word for test, נִסָּה, also means to elevate. This hints to the purpose of a test; namely, to raise the one who undergoes it to higher levels. Also, our Rabbis call the person who elevates himself a נֵס, meaning a banner. Those who work to reach high spiritual levels are a banner; they serve as an example and a source of inspiration for their environment, as well as for the generations to come.

[14] **Worms infested it** – Hashem specifically commanded that no person should keep mann from one day to the next. He then fortified this command. Worms miraculously invaded the mann that they left over. Thus, Hashem encouraged Yisrael to live with faith. He taught them that there is no advantage in keeping for tomorrow that which Hashem gives a person for today.

And Moshe told Aaron: Take a jar, and place in it a measure of mann ... for the generations to come. (Shmos 16.33)

Yirmiyahu, in his days, challenged Yisrael, "Why do you not study Torah?"

"How then will we live?" they counter challenged him.

In response he brought out this jar of mann.

"See this, your ancestors who busied themselves with Torah, lived on it. Likewise if you busy yourselves with Torah, Hashem will provide you with all your needs. (Mechilta 16.33)

Shabbos and Mann

The mann also enforces the lesson of the holy Shabbos. For on Shabbos we internalize the thought that all our sustenance comes only from Hashem. The mann on Shabbos also reflected this idea. It broke its daily pattern so that no one might profane the Shabbos on its account. This change also serves as a declaration that 'nature' is no more than Hashem's will.

On Friday ... they received double" (Devarim 16.5)

When they brought their regular rations home, they measured it and discovered that they had enough mann for the needs of the day as well as for Shabbos;[16] Hashem had blessed them. (Rashi)

On Friday they picked a double portion ... and they left it over for the next morning ... it did not rot,[17] nor were there worms in it ... and there

---

[15] **The Torah's secrets** – One who ate mann lived with agony of uncertainty. He went to bed at night 'without any food in his fridge.' On the other hand, he also experienced the ecstasy of living with miracles. Every morning he could delight anew at his breakfast falling to him from the skies. Only a person who lives such a lifestyle, with such agony and ecstasy, may truly appreciate Hashem's truth. Only such a person may penetrate the Torah's secrets.

Likewise, anyone who wishes to know the awesome truth of Hashem's Creation and the Divine will that powers it, needs to live as that generation lived. He "must throw his all on Hashem," (Tehillim 65.23), and live with faith. Then he may enter the realm of the spirit. Then he may pick up the Torah's pulse.

[16] **As well as for Shabbos** – This was the first difference; every person received on Friday twice his normal portion. A second difference was that no mann fell on Shabbos.

[17] **And it did not rot** – This was a third difference. While mann left over from one day to the next rotted, on Shabbos it remained warm and fresh. A fourth difference was that the mann on Shabbos had a different and special taste.

were people who went out on the seventh day to gather [*mann*] and they did not find any.[18] (Shmos 16.22-27)

Greed and Mann

Another lesson the mann teaches is that a person greedy for more, does not profit. Ultimately, he gets no more than he deserves to get; while his remaining efforts go to waste.

> There were those who took much, and those who took little. Yet when they came home, and measured what they had taken, they discovered that he who had taken much had no more than he who had taken little. (Shmos 16.17,18 and Rashi there)

Ingratitude

When Yisrael requested bread, Hashem accepted and fulfilled their desire with a great show of affection. However, when they demanded meat, while Hashem sent them huge amounts of flying quail, it came together with harsh punishments and tragedy. (See BaMidbar 11.5,6) What was the difference between the two?

> R' Yehoshua ben Korcha taught: They asked for meat in an unfitting way,[19] therefore they received it in an unfitting way – at night. They asked for bread in a fitting way,[20] therefore they received it in a fitting way – in the morning. (Yoma 75a)

> "Although they asked Me for meat with stomachs bulging," said Hashem, "I will give it to them;[21] so that no one may say I am unable to fulfill his desires. Still, while I give it to them now, ultimately, I will punish them for this." (Mechilta 16.12)

---

[18] **They did not find any** – Yet another miracle occurred when certain trouble-makers laid mann in the fields to discredit Shabbos's sanctity. Hashem sent birds to eat all that they had left out.

[19] **In an unfitting way** – Hashem had given them much livestock when they left Egypt, and instead of complaining, they could have slaughtered them. Also, they could have survive well enough without meat. To treat them measure for measure, Hashem gave them the quail at an unfitting time, at night – when they were already tired and it was bothersome to prepare it. Rashi

[20] **They asked for bread in a fitting way** – for a man cannot live without bread. Rashi

[21] **I will give it to them** – It is not always to our benefit, to have Hashem follow our instructions.

R' Chanina taught: The righteous ate the quail serenely, while the wicked ate it like thorns.[22] (Yoma 75b)

The Mann Tests

One other lesson the mann teaches, is that the righteous enjoy preferable treatment, while the wicked experience hardships. This discrimination is not favoritism. Rather, it is a mechanism to encourage proper behavior. Hashem wants us to learn that when we act correctly, we profit, whereas when we are selfish, spiteful and stupid, we lose.

Also this mechanism indicates to each individual 'how well he is doing' in a spiritual sense. The degree of *heavenly* blessing he enjoys, shows the sensitive soul how much Hashem likes him.

For the *tzaddikim*, the mann was [ready-to-eat] bread, for average people, it was dough [and needed baking], while for the *wicked* it [was grain, and] needed grinding in a mill. (Yoma 75a)

For the *tzaddikim*, it fell at their doorways, for average people, they had to leave their tents to fetch it; while the wicked needed to travel afar.[23] (Yoma 75b)

The *mann* would cleanse *b'nei Yisrael* of their sins. How so? When two people came before Moshe for judgment, one claiming "You stole my slave," and the other claiming, "You sold him to me," Moshe would respond, "In the morning we will know!"

If in the morning the slave's portion of mann was next to the first one's house, all could know that the second had stolen him;[24] and if it was next to the second's one home, all could know that he had bought it. (Yoma 75a)

---

[22] **Like thorns** – While the quail represented a great wealth, they were unable to enjoy it. Without Hashem's blessing, it was all like thorns.

[23] **The wicked needed to travel afar** – The more a person uses his time to serve Hashem, the more Hashem helps him arrange his personal affairs. Hashem helps him not to waste time in his mundane pursuits. Conversely, the more a person squanders the time he could use to serve Hashem, the more Hashem squanders his time. He causes him to run around in never-ending circles, never quite finishing all that he has to do.

[24] **The second had stolen him** – While people may construct great palaces of deceit, they ultimately will fall. Hashem's justice topples and demolishes them all. The mann symbolizes how Hashem uses many different agents to carry out His justice – even a person's breakfast may serve as such an agent.

GLOSSARY

Asa – A descendent King David, and himself a King of Israel.

Avram/Avraham Avinu – Abraham, the first of the patriarchs.

B'ezras Hashem – With the help of Hashem.

B'nei Yisrael – The children of Israel.

Baruch Hashem – Blessed is Hashem.

Bavel – Babylon; a home to the Jewish people for many centuries.

Beis Haknesses – A house of worship.

Beis Hamikdash – The Holy Temple that stood in Jerusalem.

Birkas Hamazon – Grace after meals.

Bocherim – Young men

Breisa – A teaching from the Mishnaic Era.

Brocha – A blessing.

Chanoch – See Genesis 5.21

Chas V'shalom – May Hashem have mercy on us and bless us with His peace.

Chashmonean – Hasmoneons, heroes of the Jewish people.

Chazon Ish – Rav Avraham Yeshayahu Karelitz (1878-1953) One of the great Torah authorities and leaders of the Jewish people.

Dinar/Dinarim – A common denomination in Gemara times.

David Hamelech – King David.

Eretz Yisrael – The land of Israel.

Erev Shabbos – The eve of the Sabbath day.

Shabbos – The Sabbath day.

Erev Yom Kippur – The eve of the Day of Atonement.

Eyn Horo – The Evil Eye, a negative spiritual force.

Gan Aden – The Garden of Eden, paradise.

Gehinom – Hell.

Gemara – The Talmud.

Geula – The redemption of the Jewish people.

Hashem – literally: The Name. A title used to refer to G-d.

Havdala – The ceremony performed at the close of Shabbos to distinguish between the holy and the profane.

Kabbala – Traditional mystical teachings.

Klal Yisrael – The assembly of Yisrael.

Kohen Gadol – The high priest.

Kohen/Kohanim – Priests who served in the holy Temple.

Kehilla – community.

Kosher – Proper and fitting.

Kollel – A group of scholars who study Torah full-time.

Levi/Leviim – The Levites whose job was to assist the Kohanim.

Lot – A nephew of our forefather, Avraham.

Maharsha – A classical commentary of the Talmud, written by R' Shmuel Eliezer (HaLevi) Idlish.

Mann – Manna. The food the Jewish people ate when they left Egypt.

Masores – Tradition.

Matza – The unleavened bread eaten on during the Passover holiday.

Mazal – Fortune.

Medrash – A homiletic teaching from the Mishnaic period.

Menora – The candelabra used in the Holy Temple.

Metzora – One afflicted with a spiritual disease resembling leprosy.

Mezuza/Mezuzos – A scroll set on the doorposts of a Jewish home.

Mishkan – Tabernacle; a portable, tent-like equivalent of the Temple.

Mishna – A teaching from the Mishnaic era.

Mitzva Matza – The matza used on the first night of Passover.

Mitzva/Mitzvos – Divine commands of Hashem.

Moshe Rabbeinu – Our teacher, Moses.

Moshiach – The Messiah.

Nisan – First month of the Jewish year; time of the grain harvest.

P'rutah – A small coin. Something like the American penny.

Parnosa – Livelihood.

Rambam – R' Moshe ben Maimon, also known as Maimonides (1135-1204). A great of Rabbinic leader, legal codifier and teacher.

Rashi – R' Shlomo ben Yitzchak (1040-1104). A leading commentator of the Bible and Talmud.

Rav/Rebbi (R') – A term of respect and honor given to a Torah scholar.

Ribis – Interest.

Rosh Hashana – The first day of the new Jewish year.

Sedom And Amora – Cities Hashem destroyed. See Genesis 18,19.

Sefer/Sifrei Torah – The scrolls with the five books of Moses.

Shabbos – The Sabbath day.

Shabbos Shiur – A lesson given of Shabbos.

Shas – A term used to describe the Talmud.

Shechita. – Ritual slaughter.

Shiur/Shiurim – Torah lessons.

Shlomo Hamelech – King Solomon, son of King David.

Shmitta – The Sabbatical year.

Shul – A term used for house of worship.

Tallis/Talleisim – A prayer shawl.

Tanach – The Bible.

Tarpik – A small coin.

Tefillin – Phylacteries.

Tishrei – The seventh month of the Jewish year; also the time for harvesting the summer fruits.

Torah – Hashem's Divine teachings.

Tosephos – A school of scholars living in France and the surrounding areas in the 12th and 13th centuries.

Tower Of Bavel – See Genesis 11.

Tzaddik/Tzaddikim – A righteous person.

Tzedaka – Charity.

Vilna Gaon – R' Eliyahu of Vilna (1720-1797). A brilliant Torah scholar and leader of the Jewish people.

Yakov – Jacob, the third of the patriarchs.

Yam Suf – The Red, or Reed Sea. The Jewish people crossed it when they left Egypt.

Yerushalayim – Jerusalem.

Yeshiva – School of Talmudic study.

Yiras Shamayim – The awe of Heaven.

Yisrael – Israel.

Yitzchak – Isaac, the second of the patriarchs.

Yoveil – The Jubilee year.

Zehuvim – Gold coins.

Zt'l – May the memory of his righteousness be a source of blessing.

Zuz/Zuzim – A common denomination used in Gemara times.

www.bnpublishing.com

www.ingramcontent.com/pod-product-compliance
Lightning Source LLC
Chambersburg PA
CBHW030614290326
41930CB00049B/386